Taste

TASTE

The Secret Meaning of Things

Stephen Bayley

Pantheon Books, New York

Library of Congress Cataloging-in-Publication Data

Bayley, Stephen.
    Taste : the secret meaning of things / by Stephen Bayley.
        p.   cm.
    Includes bibliographical references and index.
    ISBN 0-394-55892-8
    1. Aesthetics.   I. Title.
  N66.B38   1992
  701′.17—dc20   90-53399

Manufactured in the United States of America
First American Edition

To
Flo and Bruno and Coco

CONTENTS

'You know, Ward, there's only one thing that matters, only one. Is it interesting?'

Georgia O'Keeffe to Ward Bennett

'*Le secret d'ennuyer c'est de dire tout.*'

FOREWORD

In her elegant autobiography *Images and Shadows* (1970), Iris Origo, who grew up in the cultivated atmosphere of the Villa Medici near Florence, has an anecdote about her step-father, Geoffrey Scott, accomplished author of *The Architecture of Humanism* (1924). She says that Scott contemplated writing a history of taste and the whole crowd at the villa agreed this would have been a 'fascinating and enter-taining book'. Apparently, there was a great deal of conversation about it on the terraces and in the *saloni*. For weeks and weeks after the idea was mooted a sheet of paper sat on Scott's writing table. It was bravely inscribed

A History of Taste
Volume 1
Chapter 1

'It is very difficult . . .'

'So far as I know,' his stepdaughter concluded, 'the work progressed no further.'

I have come a great deal further than Geoffrey Scott, perhaps without the elegance he might have achieved, but certainly with all the difficulties he so properly anticipated. Taste is an elusive subject, since it is both a mirror and a window. Scott was probably right to stick to his poems and leave the mirrored maze unexplored.

The difficulty in writing about taste is this: any reasonably objective survey of the histories of art, manners and literature shows that taste, at least as expressed in terms of our prefer-ences, *changes*. It is demonstrably – sometimes hilariously – the case that pictures, buildings, designs, books and behaviour which find favour in one generation are perversely

Fashion is a function of time rather than of function. Fashion designers – here is Yves St-Laurent in the early 1970s – do not deal in absolutes but in momentary preferences. Their commercial success depends on their ability to be six months in front of popular taste.

The Cycle of Fashion

Indecent	10 years before its time
Shameless	5 years before its time
Outré	1 year before its time
Smart	–
Dowdy	1 year after its time
Hideous	10 years after its time
Ridiculous	20 years after its time
Amusing	30 years after its time
Quaint	50 years after its time
Charming	70 years after its time
Romantic	100 years after its time
Beautiful	150 years after its time

James Laver, *Taste and Fashion*, 1945

despised in the next. Indeed, the cycle of taste – from modishness to disfavour and then to camp revival – is a familiar one upon which the spurious dynamics of the fashion industry depend.

Accept this volatility and you accept that there can be no such things as objective 'good' taste, but only an evanescent, culturally and historically specific preference for certain things. How is the individual to determine the worth of his or her tastes in this world of continuously shifting values? Whether tastes are inherited or acquired, they will always be in question.

But are aesthetic convictions or beliefs, no matter how passionately held, as subject to the capricious depredations of time as platform soles and flared trousers? Surely some aesthetic standards survive the brief seasons of fashion? Maybe. There is a tension in this book which some will find stimulating, others irritating. It arises from the conflict between my *observation* that taste changes, that values are fugitive, and my personal *conviction* that there *are* certain forms, shapes and ideas which transcend time and have a special, permanent value. Writing this book has tested my conviction against the evidence of observation.

Exactly why is it so repugnant to learn that the Duke and Duchess of Windsor had staff to hand-cut their lavatory paper and employed a footman to feed their pug dogs meals in silver bowls? Why is it so laughable to learn that in the barrio of Villa Mora, a fashionable district of Asuncion in Paraguay, the houses are tropical-alpine kitsch? When property developer Donald Trump sends out to his friends gold-embossed dossiers on his latest pleasure palace,

Tasteful royalty – the Duke and Duchess of Windsor for ever in pursuit of a mythic gentility.

Above   Arrivistes like the disgraced Marcos family acquire the apparatus of status. There is no more certain betrayer of origins than taste. Here good manners are traded for bogus grandeur.

Right   The modern movement in architecture attempted to get beyond taste and define standards of design. Its scriptural home was the Bauhaus, where Walter Gropius's study was a shrine. There were many half-truths in modern movement theory, but no lies.

Mar-a-Lago, a 118-room villa on 20 acres in Florida, built in the 1920s of Dorian stone and shipped-in fifteenth-century Spanish tiles, in order to impress them with the dimensions and textures of his affluence, many people – particularly those, like me, schooled in the reductivist aesthetic of Modernism that until recently dominated contemporary thought – feel a revulsion so fundamental that it is tempting to call it instinctive. Incidentally, in Paraguay they also have neo-Trump architecture.

Alan Bond, the disgraced Australian billionaire, has a wife who used to cruise Perth in a pale blue Mercedes with leopard skin upholstery. When a Bond daughter married, invitations were sent out in white leather wallets which contained gold medallions embossed with the profiles of the bride and groom.

Yet there is nothing inherently 'good' or 'bad' about the Windsors', Paraguayan, Trump's or Bond's taste. Trump's dossier or Bond's invitation may be gaudy or vulgar, but, given the crassness of the attempt to impress with an ostentatious display of wealth, it would not have been more attractive had it been austerely set in Helvetica Light or Gill Sans and printed on the purest vellum, handmade by chaste Carmelite nuns. Indeed, each is probably an example of very good and effective *design*, since it achieves with surpassing ease the intention of impressing . . .

In contrast, take the architectural design of a Bauhaus room, director Walter Gropius's own study, say, so admired by people like me and yet so distant from rich and successful people like Donald Trump. Here is the most rational design the art and science of the 1920s could achieve, a monument to functionalism and the

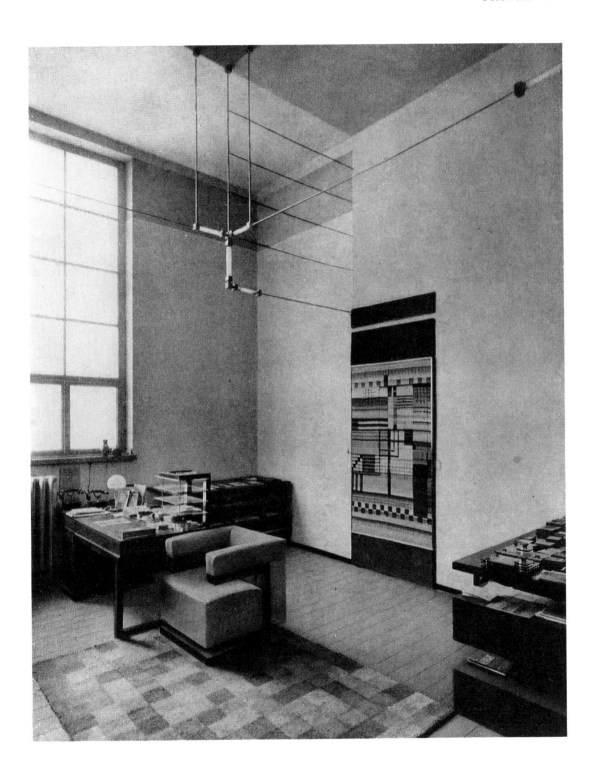

machine aesthetic that has dominated twentieth-century culture. But Walter Gropius's 'functionalism' is no more than the resolution of a circular argument that was very much of his own devising: functionalism is a good thing; geometric forms, industrial materials and primary colours are functional; therefore, geometric forms, industrial materials and primary colours are a good thing.

As the disappointing history of social housing in the Bauhaus tradition has shown, designs by Walter Gropius are fine for those like Gustav Mahler and me who enjoy mind games, and share positivist beliefs in the benefits of heliotherapy and herbalism, but are less successful when foisted on blue-collar workers whose own aspirations are to live in a blaze of polychrome vulgarity like Mr Trump.

These two examples give away something of the game. Taste is not so much about what things *look* like, as about the ideas that gave rise to them. Intention is the key to understanding taste; we must judge the spirit that informs an object or a gesture, rather than the form of the object or the gesture itself, which is a matter of *design*. It was Sigmund Freud's personal feeling for form – what his biographer Peter Gay called an 'appreciation of beauty as a kind of perfection' – that made him so uncomfortable with the style of his masterpiece, *The Interpretation of Dreams* (1898).

This book, too, is about interpretation, but it concentrates on, or rather hints at, the *meaning of things*. My own idea of perfection – sometimes unstated, often explicit – lies behind all the phenomena I single out for comment, or for more complicated criticism or praise.

While writing I have become convinced that, discounting narrow philological or etymological studies, an academic history of taste is not so much difficult as impossible. So, this book is not a history but a suggestive essay. Since a part of it was written in Italy, it seemed a good idea to divide it into two parts, somewhat like the *commedia dell'arte*. The first part is the *imbroglio*, the improvised story of an idea. The second is the *scenario*, which shows how taste has developed and changed in architecture, design, food and fashion. I will emphasize throughout how the modern question of taste is utterly dependent on the ideas of consumption fostered in industrial and post-industrial cultures. As in the *commedia dell'arte*, *lazzi* (gags) interrupt the performance, but here they take the form of pictures and their captions, rather than histrionic asides.

Taste might evade absolute definition, but we are known by our momentary expressions of choice. There is an approach to studying patterns of preference and consumption which allows the meaning of things to be interpreted: every artefact and gesture is the disguise of a meaningful structure. Taste is about consumption and, in consuming, we reveal ourselves.

Unlike Freud's, my analysis and style may not be quite equal to the task. I may lapse too easily into facetious, image-seeking circumlocations, squinting at ideas, all the while offending an inner ideal and perhaps sadly indicating an inadequate mastery of the material. Still, we are a little further on than Geoffrey Scott, with his empty sheet of foolscap and his poems.

Stephen Bayley
Vauxhall, Montestigliano and San Felice
1988–91

Part One

IMBROGLIO

TASTE

The Story of an Idea

Shakespeare and design: the shifting value of art

Look at Dr Freud's consulting rooms. The great man is sitting in a sombre Viennese interior. You can see the craquelure, smell the leather and the polish, sense the aspidistra. Even though it is a black and white photograph you can tell the dominant colour is brown. Tomes of grim Mitteilungen suggest that psychoanalysis has the sanction of the past, that it is an ancient and respected academic medical practice.

Two things would be different if Dr Freud were practising in New York or London today rather than in the volatile Vienna of Loos, Schiele, Klimt and Werfel. One is that his consulting rooms would look very different: nowadays leaders of the medical profession do not present their seriousness in terms of sombre bourgeois interior design; wealthy professionalism is suggested by black leather and chrome furniture and middlebrow junk art. The other is that the dark corners of his patients' minds would, on inspection, be found to be corroded not by anxieties about sex, death and mother (for nowadays these things are commonplace), but by . . . taste. This word, which formerly signified no more than 'discrimination', was hijacked and its meaning inflated by an influential élite who use the expression '*good* taste' simply to validate their personal aesthetic preferences while demonstrating their vulgar presumption of social and cultural superiority. The very idea of good taste is insidious. While I stop short of believing that all human affairs are no more than a jungle of ethical and cultural relativity, the suggestion that the infinite variety and vast sweep of the mind should be

The professions have traditionally required imagery to buttress their status, especially in their offices. Dr Freud chose sombre academicism, but a successful modern doctor prefers his surgery to look like an Italian furniture showroom.

limited by some polite mechanism of 'good form' is absurd.

Everyone has taste, yet it is more of a taboo subject than sex or money. The reason for this is simple: claims about your attitudes to or achievements in the carnal and financial arenas can be disputed only by your lover and your financial advisers, whereas by making statements about your taste you expose body and soul to terrible scrutiny. Taste is a merciless betrayer of social and cultural attitudes.[1] Thus, while anybody will tell you as much as (and perhaps more than) you want to know about their triumphs in bed and at the bank, it is taste that gets people's nerves tingling.

Nancy Mitford noted in her acute discussion of the term 'common' (as in 'He's a common

Nancy Mitford, waspish author of *Noblesse Oblige*, was a ferocious snob. The daughter of Lord Redesdale was brought up in surroundings of superb antiquarian glamour. Such environments cultivate lethargy in matters of taste.

little man') that it is common even to use the word 'common', which gives double-bluffers rich hunting grounds among the maladroit and insecure. Explicit social class and explicit material taste are a part of the post-industrial re-ordering of the world and as Nick Furbank wittily pointed out in his book about snobbery, *Unholy Pleasures* (1985), 'in classing someone socially, one is simultaneously classing oneself'. He might just as easily have said 'in criticizing someone else's taste, one is simultaneously criticizing oneself'.

The one certain thing about taste is that it changes. Taste began to be an issue when we lost the feeling for intelligible natural beauty possessed by the Neoplatonists and medieval artists and writers. Nature and art are, in a sense, opposites, and art has been the most reliable barometer of attitudes to beauty. As André Malraux noted at the end of the 1940s, in the modern world, art, even religious art of the past, is divorced from its religious purposes and has become a negotiable commodity for consumption by rich individuals or by museums.

Art was the first 'designer' merchandise and there is no surer demonstration of fluctuating taste than the reputations of the great artists and the pictures they created. Averaged across centuries of first lionization and then neglect, it is clear that these reputations have no permanent value: the estimation of the value of art depends as much on the social and cultural conditions of a particular viewer as on qualities embodied in the work itself.

The reputation of El Greco is the paradigm of this phenomenon. Praised in his own lifetime, he painted in a style, exaggerated even by the standards of mannerism, which neo-

The El Greco monument in Sitges. Famous in his own lifetime, ignored a century later, reviled just after that and then spontaneously revived, El Greco is now considered an 'old master'. There is no better example of the impermanent value of art than his fugitive reputation.

'The collecting of art is not about taste and caution; it is about style and courage.'

Alistair McAlpine, 1991

classical critics found unsettling. The only way encyclopedists could interpret his attenuated forms and his spooky colours was to claim he was going blind and had gone mad. A century later, French Romantics travelling in Spain, like Théophile Gautier, recognized in El Greco's forms, colours and mannerisms exactly those passions they wanted to versify, paint or articulate. Half a century on Picasso singled El Greco out for major cultural rehabilitation.[2]

Once El Greco could only be understood in terms of medically recognizable disorders, but by the early twentieth century he was seen in a more positive, less pathological light and hailed as a source of *duende*, the romantic Spanish gloominess described by Lorca. This *duende* inspired Picasso: his *Les Demoiselles d'Avignon*, conventionally held to be the origin of Cubism, was as much influenced by El Greco as by Cézanne and allowed Picasso to claim an earlier Spanish precedent for the movement he invented. As El Greco became a cult, other converts followed Picasso, including his friend Santiago Rusinol, a rich aesthete responsible for the Catalan Renaixenca.[3]

As arbiters of taste are inclined to, Rusinol created a museum, Cau Ferrat, in Sitges in 1894 to vindicate his own preferences. In the opening ceremony his two El Greco paintings were carried on a float to the accompaniment of a marching band while assistants scattered flowers. By 1898 Rusinol had convinced his fellow townsmen to subscribe to a monument to the painter, which still stands in the Catalan port. At the same time, Picasso's studio was covered with photographs of El Greco, and in fact close parallels in both style and subject matter can be seen between Blue Period Picasso

Fine art is as subject to the depredations of time as high fashion. When El Greco painted like Titian he was accepted, but his later distortions gave him a reputation for madness. Three centuries later, Picasso was favourably influenced by the very paintings the neo-classicists had repudiated.

Gilbert Scott's Albert Memorial has been labelled a 'test for taste'. It won an architectural competition against other entries, including an Albert Fountain, but was ridiculed even before it was finished. By the early twentieth century it was considered grotesque, but the revival of interest in Victoriana (beginning *c*.1958) turned it into a much-loved monument.

and late El Greco. The identification of one with the other went so far that in one sketch-book Picasso scribbled, 'Yo el Greco, yo el Greco' (I am El Greco, I am El Greco).

El Greco is now established as an 'old master' after centuries of alternating vilification and neglect. Or is he? The El Greco anecdote makes clear that what is fashionable in one generation often becomes preposterous in the next. When Kenneth Clark wrote his first book, *The Gothic Revival* (1928), it was almost as a *jeu d'esprit*: Victorian Gothic architecture was a lost cause and it was a sophisticated and amusing literary rite of passage for a parvenu aesthete such as Clark to talk it up.

During the First World War, on strolls through Kensington Gardens, the philosopher R. G. Collingwood was shocked by the ugliness of the Albert Memorial. He concluded in his *Autobiography* (1939) that the Albert Memorial was 'visibly misshapen, corrupt, crawling, verminous'. Despite this attack, he found the general effect of Gilbert Scott's design so powerful that he produced a study, *Truth and Contradiction*, which attempted to deal with the perplexing problems, perceptual and ideological, which the curious memorial caused him. A marvellous diversion in the history of taste, it was never published.

The Albert Memorial has often been described as a 'test for taste'. Despite Collingwood's obloquy, the memorial became absorbed into the repertoire of Englishness, while the memory of the cruel and squalid age which created it faded into comfortable nostalgia. The Gothic revival itself, witness the successive editions of Clark's book, became more and more acceptable, until verminous became quaint and quaint became haunting. This process culminated in the founding of the Victorian Society in 1958, a club whose members can also be verminous, quaint and haunting.

Perhaps an even more dramatic demonstration of changing values in art occurs in literature. Shakespeare's reputation as a genius of timeless relevance is a recent one, or, at least, recently renewed. To us he bestrides the narrow world like a colossus. And so he did to Samuel Sheppard, who in 1651 described him as 'sacred', but by 1662 Samuel Pepys thought *Romeo and Juliet* 'the worst [(play] that I ever heard' and described *A Midsummer Night's Dream* as 'insipid' and 'ridiculous'. Half a century later Alexander Pope called Shakespeare 'divine', but there was also a moment in the eighteenth century when he was regarded as a talented barbarian of local interest and little more: Dr Johnson wrote in the 1765 Preface to his edition of Shakespeare that he 'has . . . faults, and faults sufficient to obscure and overwhelm any other merit.' Voltaire likened Shakespeare's complete works to a 'dunghill'. Thomas Bowdler found Shakespeare so offensive that in 1807 and 1818 he edited the works for family consumption, so that 'Satan's cleverest bait' would no longer drag pure-minded youth towards a life of vice. Bernard Shaw despised him and Tolstoy wrote of 'an insuperable repulsion and tedium' on reading *King Lear*, *Romeo and Juliet* and *Hamlet*.

Civilization has presumably not reached such a degree of global stagnation that the value of Shakespeare might not again be reassessed, and, in an age with different (although perhaps not superior) values, his literary art

We are all influenced by the taste of our times. If Keats were writing today, his subject would be cars or planes.

might be found wanting. The ebbs and flows of history show us that the possibility exists. If great artists and playwrights are vulnerable, what claims can be made for *design*?

More than mere historical anecdote, this spectre of continuous reassessment suggests an extraordinary dynamism, even uncertainty, perhaps even arbitrariness, in matters of aesthetic judgement, affecting everything from altarpieces to washing machines. Another example: the poet John Keats was fascinated by Hellenism. In a library somewhere in Rome or London he focused on an engraving of the British Museum's Townley vase (or some say the engravings of the Borghese vase in the Louvre) and wrote of his 'still unravish'd bride of silence' that 'Beauty is truth, truth beauty'.[4]

Beauty and truth bring together the formal and the moral, just as the acknowledgement of the existence of taste requires us to judge one in terms of the other: formality and morality might also be used to describe the purposes of modern industrial design. A Bauhaus teapot, for instance, is both a geometry lesson and a sermon.

The apparent universality and implied timelessness of Keats's judgement is made less clear and more poignant by the clutter of metaphor surrounding the poem. In trying to come to terms with the problem of beauty and decay (a concern of other poems, including 'Ode on Melancholy' and 'Ode to a Nightingale'), and, 'saddened by the mutability of natural beauty, he sought consolation in the more permanent beauty of art'.[5] But the perception of value in art changes.

A century and more nearer our own time the pioneer American design consultant Norman Bel Geddes, addressing the spirit of the age, claimed that if Keats had been writing in 1940 he would have said the same about an aeroplane as he had about that old Grecian urn. In the Middle Ages the scholastic philosophers construed beauty to be an attribute of God, rather than of urns or aeroplanes; beauty and art were not necessarily related, indeed the idea of 'art' as a discrete activity was not acknowledged.[6] Keats's neo-classicism, the prevailing taste of his day, required him to admire the Hellenic pot, while Norman Bel Geddes, suffused with the spirit of the twentieth century, was as moved by the plane. In *Design This Day* Geddes's contemporary, Walter Dorwin Teague, apparently without irony, compared one of the Texaco filling stations he had designed to the temples of Greece.

Each age finds its own expression in material things and the faculty we use to identify those we find palatable or repellent we call taste. With the spread of materialism, consumerism and commodity fetishism, minute aesthetic criteria are being established as the basis for general social competition for the first time in civilization. Everyday things we consume are – if perhaps only briefly – acquiring the sombre resonance of great art.

Because it involves everything we do, taste can soon become a neurosis. Just as quality in design is most conveniently explained by the use of moralizing terms like honest, decent and sound, which have their origins in observations of human behaviour, taste is similarly rooted in performance, in that the exercise of it is somewhat akin to manners.[7] The architect Viollet-le-duc, an eloquent spokesman for structural rationalism in building design,

Your possessions tell revealing stories about you. Best to appear what you are, not what you would wish to be. Best also to leave your Mercedes-Benz uncustomized. More is worse.

applied the same principles to personal behaviour, believing that, '*Le goût consiste en paraître ce que l'on est, et non ce que l'on voudrait être.*'

Semantically, taste is rich and confusing, its etymology as odd and interesting as that of 'style'. But while style – deriving from the stylus or pointed rod which Roman scribes used to make marks on wax tablets – suggests activity, taste is more passive. The old Latin tag '*De gustibus non est disputandum*' (there is no disputing about taste) is the oldest formulation of the idea 'One man's meat is another man's poison'. It is primary evidence that since Roman days the matter of taste has involved choice, whether individual or collective. Today, taste means both aesthetic and social discrimination, as well as gustatory sensation.

Etymologically, the word we use derives from the old French, meaning touch or feel, a sense that is preserved in the current Italian word for a keyboard, *tastiera*.

In English, the term 'good taste', meaning 'sound understanding', appears in the early fifteenth century, but it is not until the seventeenth century that the concept of aesthetic discrimination arrived in England: in the 1685 translation of Baltasar Gracian's *El Oraculo Manual y Arte de Prudentia* (1647) the term '*gusto relevante*' becomes 'quaint and critical judgement'. Interestingly, this book for the courtier has never been out of print since its first appearance, and, more interestingly still for a book devoted to the professional cultivation of *charm*, it was made most famous in the German translation of Arthur Schopenhauer.

The metaphorical use of 'taste' to mean judgement began in France, where Gracian's '*gusto relevante*' was rendered as '*le goût fin*'. A literal translation gave a new and troublesome word to English. The salons of France, where art, literature, antiquities and science were discussed in circumstances of considerable comfort and luxury, adopted the word and gave it a capital 'T'.

By the early eighteenth century the word 'taste' was becoming familiar in essays on literature; the major transformation was complete and 'taste' had become synonymous with judgement. A subtle and even elusive concept was born, elements of refinement and restraint attaching themselves to the definition only later.[8]

The Earl of Shaftesbury's *Letter Concerning Design* is a typical marker of the phenomenon.[9]

It was published just as critical discernment was about to become an intellectual sport. The *Letter* was written when art had been separated from its didactic and divine purposes and was well on the way to becoming a consumer product. At this moment taste did not have any particular values: it was only identified as a part of the human apparatus of discernment; you either had it or you didn't and there was no question of 'good' or 'bad'.

When man replaced God as the chief object of study, it was inevitable that the idea of beauty deriving from divine inspiration was replaced by a more secular, even materialistic, notion of aesthetic satisfaction. La Rochefoucauld remarked that 'Our pride is more offended by attacks on our tastes than on our opinions', an observation which puts into nice equilibrium the forces of cupidity and sophistication which dominate modern consumer behaviour.[10]

But in a culture which had only one class with the economic capacity to make discriminating judgements, the matter of whether taste was 'good' or 'bad' was not so much irrelevant as inconceivable and its characteristics still wanted defining. Early pursuit of precision in this matter began by trying to locate where exactly in the body taste operated. To the Earl of Shaftesbury (1671–1713), having taste was like having an accessory for the soul. To Joseph Addison (1672–1719), as soon as taste was established, vice and ignorance would automatically be banished, presumably from loins *and* head – in that order.

David Hume (1711–86) – who had said of Shakespeare 'a reasonable propriety of thought he cannot for any time uphold' – defined taste as a 'sensibility' to every kind of beauty or deformity. Hume's view was that standards *could* be established, while Sir Joshua Reynolds (1723–92) upheld this view in the fine arts. Reynolds thought that genius and taste were very much the same thing, except that genius had the added ingredient of execution. To an academic painter like Reynolds, taste was to be found lurking in the same dominion as reason and was, therefore, in his view, equally exempt from any possibility of change.

The *Discourses* which Sir Joshua Reynolds delivered at the Royal Academy between 1769 and 1786 are a *tour de force* of aesthetic conviction; they are also the richest ground for sniffing out the English Enlightenment's attitude both to man-made rules and to God-given

In the late eighteenth century, to have taste was to belong to a club. There were no variations and nothing was in doubt. Standards of taste in art were generally agreed by the academies. In the industrial world this unanimity has been lost.

The Faculties of the Mind

Perception
Memory
Imagination
Taste
Judgement

'Taste – whose office it is to determine and pronounce upon whatever is beautiful, elegant, sublime, pleasing, or the reverse of these . . . [Taste then] submits her performance to Judgement.'

William Thompson, *An Enquiry into the Elementary Principle of Taste*, 1768

genius. Reynolds declared, 'Could we teach taste or genius by rules, they would no longer be taste or genius' (1770). But in grandly stating the case for rules, he made the most persuasive statement ever of the academic principle:

Every opportunity therefore, should be taken to discountenance that false and vulgar opinion that rules are the fetters of genius. They are fetter only to men of no genius; as that armour, which upon the strong becomes an ornament and a defence, upon the weak and misshapen turns into a load and cripples the body which it was meant to protect . . . How much liberty may be taken to break through those rules . . . may be an after consideration when the pupils become masters themselves. It is then, when their Genius had received its utmost improvement, that rules may possibly be dispensed with. But let us not destroy the scaffold until we have raised the building. (1769)

Yet the worm of analysis kept burrowing in the foundation of Reynolds's classical certainties. 'How', you can imagine him always nagging himself, 'do we objectify our preferences?' Taste-makers of the eighteenth century were concerned with whether judgements were based on mysterious, internal forces insusceptible to analysis, or whether there was a standard of taste which was rational and measurable, which could be scientifically determined and from which no reasonable man would withhold his approval. In this transition from the classic to the romantic in art, David Hume suggested that beauty was not solely subjective to the viewer, but may be inherent in objects.

This suspicion was reinforced by Immanuel Kant (1724–1804), who reasoned that aesthetic judgements have universal validity. Kant was wrong.

An explosion in production during the nineteenth century opened up consumption to social classes which did not include the President of the Royal Academy and distinguished philosophers; the idea of taste then came to represent not a commonly held view, but the antithesis of choices made in the market-place, which, patronizing experts always observed, expressed themselves in a debased and depraved form. In the fine arts this meant that painters were caught in the cross-fire between Romanticism and popular culture.

The entire history of painting after, say, 1830 can be understood in terms of the dilemma faced by painters: whether to be society's picture-makers, or to be misunderstood private visionaries. Dostoevsky described this as the choice between lofty suffering and cheap happiness. Similarly, manufacturers and designers did not know whether to satisfy existing popular taste, or to lead it by enhancing it. The question has not been resolved in the fine or the applied arts, but one thing is certain: by about 1850 it was very clear that aesthetic judgements – wheresoever applied and by whom – most certainly did not have universal validity. The age of consumerism has no time for Kant.

To account for this popular rejection of severe philosophy, the aspirational concept of 'good' taste began to emerge. Good taste was assumed to be a standard to which the masses would aspire, were they given the chance. The legacy of this underpins our behaviour in every

Immanuel Kant searched for the basis of aesthetic motivation. For such a difficult journey, Königsberg was not a good place to start.

Above   In the mid-twentieth century the notion of 'good design' – usually represented by prim Scandinavian furniture – was advanced by art magazines and architecture schools. It was an unscientific nostrum, a means of formalizing the tastes of a liberal élite.

Right   The 'good design' movement, which depended on certain types of merchandise being approved for consumption, achieved its *reductio ad absurdum* in the 'designer' phenomenon, which began in the late 1970s when Gloria Vanderbilt was persuaded to put her signature on otherwise unremarkable jeans.

activity from interior decorating to eating and table manners. Art historians have long struggled to understand what Birmingham manufacturers in the 1840s and shopkeepers of the 1980s understand intuitively: the mechanism by which civilizations and their preferences change and evolve.

Cultural historians, in pursuit of meaning in the chaos of history, take refuge in vague structural models such as Hegel's *Volksgeist*, an abstract entity embodying the national spirit, which imparts a common stamp to religion, politics, ethics, customs, arts and science. Marxism substituted economic conditions for the *Zeitgeist*, spirit of the age, but

the frigid calculations of the political economists do not clarify the nebulous discussion.
Mixed industrial economies substituted 'good'
design for Marxist imperatives.

In an address to the Danish Society of Industrial Design in 1970, J. K. Galbraith said: 'As
living standards rise – as man multiplies the
goods he consumes and the artifacts with
which he surrounds himself – we are entitled
to believe, or at least to hope, that quantitative
measurements give way to qualitative ones.' A
vain hope, since economists have no explanation for the mechanism of choice, even if its
consequences are the very stuff of economics.
How does change in taste affect supply and
demand? How does a change in income distri-
bution alter the ability of a market to satisfy
certain tastes? But taste itself always lies out

there . . . it is exogenous, unexamined. In their
search for a value-free science economists
prefer to regard taste as a mystery, its nature
only glimpsed through 'revealed preferences':
choices registered in the market-place. Economists rarely analyse, still less judge, the origins of taste, preferring to leave it to those of
us who are less squeamish about the unquanti-
fiable.

Whatever happened to 'good' design?

Good design was an inevitable consequence of
the invention of taste. And soon after 'good'
design got itself a bad name, the word
'designer' was mired in putrid froth. The first
signs were to appear on Gloria Vanderbilt's
bottom. Indian jeans manufacturer Murjani
knew there was no better way to tart up his

product than having a famous name on them, so he pursued and failed to acquire the services of Jackie Onassis. Second choice was mature socialite Vanderbilt, who, in a contract which will form future case studies in business schools, agreed to model the product and have her signature embroidered on the rump. Thus, in one hideous, meretricious swagger of the marketing mechanism, 'designer' jeans were born.

As I write, the editors of the *Oxford English Dictionary* are engaged in tracing the descent of a word that once signified an honourable vocation. While they work, 'designer' declines still further. A lurid concoction of narcotics, hallucinogens and amphetamines was recently and witlessly described by the *Guardian* as a 'designer' drug. Someone recently started calling Perrier 'designer' water. Now anything offered for sale that is irrelevant, matt black, expensive or just plain freaky weird is sold as a designer this or a designer that. So, a vocational term for a dignified profession, which includes Vitruvius, Christopher Wren, Thomas Sheraton, Henry Ford and Eric Gill, has been debased to a slap-on epithet of no real meaning to join other dead or dying labels like 'de luxe', 'executive' and 'turbo'.

Such epithets are dead or dying because they are stripped of real meaning. When language loses its basis in reality we are threatened by suffocation in a Babel of flashy values. Car manufacturers of the 1950s and 1960s, cynically refusing to improve the suspension, transmission or engine, added cute bits and big mark-ups to banal products and called them 'de luxe', as though a Vauxhall dealer could sell you a motorized Dunlop-borne pleasure

In America the general public was always more sceptical about 'good' design than in Europe. Indeed, since the US economy, so wedded to Detroit, was committed to the annual model change (or planned obsolescence) assumptions of eternal 'good' design were undermined. American taste reached Britain not only in the form of Pop Art but also in the form of Ford and Vauxhall cars. Here c.1960, is the touching absurdity of a suburbanized dream car outside Ye Olde Tea Shoppe.

Words are debased when misapplied. 'De luxe' became a redundant term when attached to chromium-plated barges. No one dares nowadays be an 'executive' lest (s)he be confused with a briefcase or a calculator; 'turbo' applies to polish and aftershave. 'Designer' has followed this descending path.

dome instead of an under-engineered barge that droned, squeaked, smelt of plastic and made you feel sick. The ghost of meaning attached to the concept 'executive briefcase' is exorcized as soon as you articulate it. 'Turbo', a word once used exclusively by researchers into forced induction in heat engines, is now liberally applied to anything from chocolate to carpet shampoo, though the sweets and the soap are not fitted with an exhaust-driven compressor.

The absurd debasement of the 'designer' is a fascinating episode in the history of taste, and all the more extraordinary when you consider that only a little earlier this century 'design' began to usurp art in its power to delight and astonish the public. As soon as painters and sculptors ceased to communicate with people and chose instead to create commodities of debatable artistic interest exclusively for dealers and museums, it was inevitable that the public would take its aesthetic pleasures where it could find them: in the styling of cars, the cinema and in popular culture. Put another way, the century of consumerism has moved the entire man-made world into the province of aestheticism.

With the whole of material culture open to

scrutiny and painting disappearing up its own art, it was necessary to make some claims for design. One of the first consisted of certain learned people declaring certain artefacts to be in possession of that mysterious and numinous attribute 'good' design. Good design could mean something as long as there was some identifiable competition in the form of 'bad' design. In Britain and the US in the 1950s and 1960s there was felt to be more of one than the other, and it perhaps meant something because then you found lots of manufacturers competing in the same field, some making good design and some bad. But 'good design' was rarely defined precisely, because what was really being discussed was not so much design of any sort as taste. No survivors of the period are willing to confirm this devastating observation,

The design establishment has retained a lingering capacity to moralize, in the face of a lack of popular interest. Few of its representatives will acknowledge that its efforts are, on the whole, expressions of a taste as evanescent as that for velvet trousers or wax fruit.

but you can still hear them, like J. K. Galbraith, pointing to bleached ash Scandinavian furniture with webbing seats, products and typefaces in certain reductivist forms, colours of a certain restraint, and saying, with the fervour of the fundamentalist, 'That is good design.' Maybe, maybe not, but what they almost certainly mean is, 'For someone of my age and educational background, that is to my taste.' In other words, 'I know better than you.'

This sort of 'goodness' began to discredit design in the eyes of the public, because it suggested the exclusivity of a remote clique. There is excellence in design, but it is altogether more scientific: you can measure it and weigh it. You know for certain when something is durable, affordable, useful, efficient and – if you make it – profitable. What is less certain is whether you like it, whether bleached ash furniture tells other people things about you which you would like them to know. Does it reveal the social and cultural influences operating on you? Is it sending the world secret messages about you? Does it betray your . . . taste?

Good design got itself a bad name because of this confusion, and the 'designer' phenomenon is an inevitable consequence of it. Just as the qualifying adjective 'good' was plucked from universal vocabulary to give extra validity to certain products, so nowadays, in the de luxe, executive, turbo tradition, 'designer' has become a tag of dubious cachet. It is, as Marxists will tell you, just one way that capitalists valorize surplus and make you think you want to consume something you don't really need. If, to paraphrase Dorothy Parker, you want to know what God thinks about 'designer' merchandize, just look at the people he gives it to.

But politics and religion aside, the 'designer' fad only survives because of credulous consumers, uncertain of their taste, adrift in oceans of junk. The depravity of the 'design' business is the implied suggestion that only jeans and mineral water and expensive things are designed – that it is rare and exclusive for something to be designed.

Everything has been designed, sometimes well, often badly, and the great challenge for manufacturers, retailers and educators is to learn to speak the language of objects so that more genuinely good design can be more widely available.

Both 'good' design and the 'designer' phenomenon are products of cynical ages, concepts which could only be validated by the continued existence of and demand for the bogus. According to J. K. Galbraith: 'It is said by the exponents of bureaucratic method that they serve the taste of the majority, and that taste is intrinsically bad. It will, indeed, be bad if there is no alternative, but given a choice, people have . . . a greater instinct for beauty than we often imagine.' With better products in all the shops neither 'good' design nor designer goods would be necessary, or even possible. But how is the individual to determine quality, or is discrimination to be merely a whim?

If we agree with Keats that beauty is itself variable, we are left with the perplexing conclusion that truth too is not eternally valid, but a function of specific social and cultural circumstances. Any dire ramifications arising from this are properly the province of philosophers and priests, but there are also implications for designers and consumers.

Clearly, in any particular age there is a

universe of choice in matters of colour, form, style and purpose, yet only certain options are generally considered worthwhile. Standards are always being established by outstanding minds in each generation. In the eighteenth century an oligarchic control of wealth influenced all aesthetic judgements and these aristocratic requirements influenced society as a whole. Nowadays, different forces operate and our understanding of them is impaired by our confusion about the difference between taste and design.

Take any object. If you have access to data you can immediately tell whether it can be manufactured economically, whether it is durable, popular and profitable. These things can be measured in dollars and centimetres. It is the less tangible elements in any design which are the subject of this book. Why do certain designs seem to transcend fashion and achieve a timeless quality?

Is it true that the form of the most admired designs is such that you can immediately understand what the object does? Is it true that in all excellent design there is a harmony and coherence between the overall form and the individual details? Do all admired products, buildings and fashions have a certain equilibrium between the technique employed in the manufacture and the intention of the product?

My intention is not to say that any taste is 'good' or 'bad', but in the midst of arguments that suggest aesthetic judgements are liable to continuous review, can any claim be made for universality? Certainly, the Modern movement can be interpreted as an attempt to restore rules to the theory and practice of architecture after a century and more of eclecticism. For perhaps

Dieter Rams, the German industrial designer whose landmark work for the Braun electrical company makes him the last survivor of the modern movement. Rams, the chief stylist of the *Wirtschaftswunder*, was given to sermonizing about the austerely beautiful forms he produced.

The Modernist Creed

'To me good design means as little design as
    possible.
Simple is better than complicated.
Quiet is better than confusion.
Quiet is better than loud.
Unobtrusive is better than exciting.
Small is better than large.
Light is better than heavy.
Plain is better than coloured.
Harmony is better than divergency.
Being well balanced is better than being
    exalted.
Continuity is better than change.
Sparse is better than profuse.
Neutral is better than aggressive.
The obvious is better than that which must be
    sought.
Few elements are better than many.
A system is better than single elements.'

Dieter Rams, 1987

fifty years of the twentieth century the modern aesthetic, disguised mostly under a veil of 'rationalism' blown stiff by the wind of social purpose, dominated European and American taste.

No one can state better the rules of that aesthetic than the German product designer Dieter Rams. A student of Ulm's austere post-war Hochschule für Gestaltung, the designer whose work for Braun made first the white and then the black box a fetishistic commodity, Rams explained his philosophy of form: '*Einfach ist besser als kompliziert. Leise ist besser als laut. Naheliegendes ist besser als Gesuchtes.*' Perhaps Dieter Rams would not accept that his version of 'simplicity' (*Einfach*), his version of 'quietness' (*Leise*) and his interpretation of 'obvious' (*Naheliegendes*) are themselves determined by aesthetic preference, and can make no claim to being undeviating absolutes. The preferences which Rams so artfully and eloquently expressed in his severely beautiful, but very restricted, designs for Braun appliances betray the social and cultural conditioning of the *Wirtschaftswunder*: they represent the *Zeitgeist*. Or did.

Different times demand different values. Nancy Mitford thought it was vulgar to display any sign of undue haste and therefore sent only business letters by airmail, whereas Dieter Rams travels the autobahns in his very fast Porsche 930. The global electronic village is not yet upon us, but clearly Nancy Mitford would have been very perturbed by a facsimile machine.

With all the past immediately available for consumption and history deregulated by postmodernism, with the world becoming smaller and smaller, taste more than ever is confused with fashion and with design.

Consuming taste

As a metaphor for choice – if not for sensation in the mouth – taste is a peculiarly modern, Western faculty. The hieratic societies of the ancient past and of the Orient did not fret about the finer points of discernment. Even in the European Middle Ages the concept did not exist. Medieval economies were based on survival and subsistence, while medieval art was didactic. The idea of art devoted to the excitement of pleasure is a recent one. Although medieval scholars had a great deal to say about proper social conduct, in a world that was not materialistic, their strictures were largely confined to canons of behaviour rather than consumerist choice.

But there are some interesting examples in the Middle Ages of things being acquired for edification and delight rather than for survival. Museums did not exist, but certain aristocrats acquired collections of curiosities as booty, as symbols of power and as hedges against economic disaster. Intended for private contemplation rather than public education, such collections are not to be understood as art; no great distinction was made between the beautiful and the merely odd. If the inventory is anything to go by, the Duc de Berry seems to have held in equal regard his collection of paintings and his embalmed elephant.

With art and life seen as one, medievals did not distinguish between the moral and the aesthetic content of works of art. Hence disinterested aesthetic experience did not exist and

therefore taste had no meaning before the beginning of the world of the consumer some four hundred years later. Beatrice Webb, aware of the modern citizen's preoccupation with being a consumer, described this role as perhaps 'the most pregnant and important piece of classification in the whole range of sociology'.[11]

Taste is in the soul of the consumer, a means of accommodating ideas about art and morality into lives which provide for little of either. Whenever we find that art and morality are in conflict, it is because we are trying to reconcile a modern conception of the aesthetic with a medieval conception of the moral.[12] The structure of modern society – where consumption of artefacts has replaced the inheritance of them – required a concept of taste so that qualitative discussion, and social competition, could present established values – definite concepts by which performance could be judged and found impressive or wanting.

Taste may be an expression of personal values, but it also identifies an individual with a certain class. Since taste was invented by and for the middle classes, it is always the middle classes who suffer in discussion of it. 'Bourgeois' is French for middle class. Once meaning merely a town person, the word had acquired a pejorative sense as early as the seventeenth century: in Molière's *Le bourgeois gentilhomme* (1670) being a town-dweller – when the court resided elsewhere – was clearly a social disadvantage. Although the term '*bourgeois*' fell into disuse during the French Revolution and was replaced by the less value-laden and more scientific '*citoyen*', British writers preserved the concept for stigmatization well into the nineteenth century.

In his *Book of Snobs* (1848), slyly subtitled 'by one of them', Thackeray calls snobbishness a 'diabolical invention of gentility', but puts gentility on the spot now and for ever more when he cautions that 'Stinginess is snobbish, ostentation is snobbish, too great profusion is snobbish.' Thackeray immediately identified patterns and preferences of consumption with moral values. Matthew Arnold in *Culture and Anarchy* (1869) described the middle class as 'Philistines' prey to 'hideous and grotesque illusions' and inclined to seduction by 'worldly splendour, security, power and pleasure', an observation since validated by the glossy magazines and their advertisers.

In 1872 when the Midland Railway decided on a two-class system in its coaches, it was

Marx introduced the word 'class' at just the time when technical innovations deriving from industrialization were partitioning society. Nowhere was this distinction more explicit than in the class system of the railways. Taste had been universal; now there was one for each class, if not for each individual.

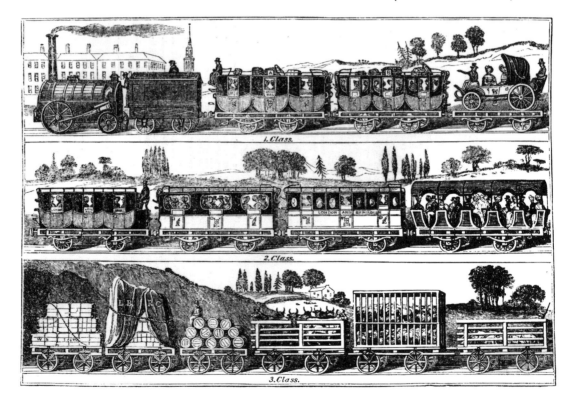

second class that went – first and third remained, the idea being to distance the one and suggest a level of aspiration for the other. Such tensions underpin the neatly constructed world of the consumer. Taste and class are almost inseparable. The greater part of economic activity in the West is devoted either to the pursuit of taste or to the disguise of class. It is the prosperous but unsure middle classes who are the most voracious consumers and therefore the ones most animated by considerations of taste.

To judge by the advertising, taste is at the heart of personal motivation in matters of consumption. Ideas about group membership and group exclusion are either overt or esoteric in most consumer advertising and in the consumption which follows it. An account at Henri Bendel's New York store was once considered a requirement for Manhattan's 'contemporary aristocracy', which *New York* magazine defined more precisely, if less attractively, as 'small-boned women who lived for style'. When the down-market chain store The Limited took over, that small-boned aristocracy was scandalized. The Jewish princess is perhaps contemporary America's most accurate gauge of taste: deracinated, classless except for levels of consumption, proud by acquisition, a keen supporter of the 'arts and diseases', patron of designers, maker and breaker, arbiter of taste.

Taste and class feed off each other. Both words and concepts, each more impressionistic than scientific, came into being and use at about the same time. In Samuel Richardson's novel *Clarissa* (1748) class supersedes the earlier 'station' and by the later eighteenth century

The pursuit of taste is one aspect of the disguise of class which motivates much commercial and social activity in the West. The modern shop represents a museum of costume and attributes.

expressions such as 'of the lowest class' were, so to speak, common. The same semantic shift took place in Germany where Karl Marx, for whom such considerations were a profession, began using *Klasse* to signify what had previously been known as *Stand* (estate). Marx said that class could only be understood in terms of an individual's relationship to the means of production (which is to say, as worker, consumer or owner). Taste can only be understood in terms of individuals' relationship to their need for consumption.

The creative people in advertising agencies are unconsciously aware that discrimination is a stimulus to consumption. The account planners are more alive to it. But their taste too is culturally determined, as any anthropologist with a global perspective can explain (or as any review of international campaigns for identical products will demonstrate). But colours, like ways of selling booze and cars, have different meanings in different territories. In Britain black is culturally associated with death and mourning, while in Venice or Spain it suggests grandeur and the grandee. Yellow is a sacred colour in China, but white is disagreeable for the same reasons that black used to be in Victorian Britain. European normality is merely a local preference. Martini is not in every sense a global product, and the technological criteria which obsess Audi engineers are no more universal a taste than *Wurst mit Rösti*. In his essay 'Reading Things' (1976), Umberto Eco asked, 'If Vienna had been on the equator and its bourgeoisie had gone around in Bermuda shorts, would Freud have described the same neurotic symptoms?' Probably not. Even here in Europe, the history of evolving social

taboos, whether bare knees or nose-picking, demonstrates a susceptibility to change. To use Nick Furbank's illustration of the absurdities of discrimination which make the English upper classes such a rich source for critical observers: 'Lord Beauchamp thought it middle-class *not* to decant champagne.'[13] Lord Beauchamp clearly had it in for the town-dwellers.

There are differences in tastes between different territories, as well as between social classes. The French have a more marked preference for offal than the Germans. In Chiavari, Italy, you can eat fish brains in the most expensive restaurants; try to serve them in Cleveland, Ohio, and you would be prosecuted by the Food and Drug Administration. There is also the element of time: taboos about food are in some cases recent. There is more than one nineteenth-century cookery book which gives instructions on how to carve a calf's eyes. With the industrialization of food-processing (and the distancing of the consumer which that process entailed) a taboo about identifiable bits of edible animals evolved: generalized meat of no specific source was safe for middle-class consumption, but an all-too-obvious eyeball, ear, snout or trotter became unacceptable. By an interesting process of inversion, this particular taboo has been reversed, so that steak and chips is, at least in England, a proletarian dish and a lamb's pancreas an extremely sophisticated one.

European culture became refined through the practice of such arcane discrimination. Since the Middle Ages, when eating and drinking were even more social spectacles than they are today, conduct at table was a ground for scholars to pontificate. In his magnificent book

The Civilising Process (1978), Norbert Elias describes medieval texts which feature discourses on socially acceptable behaviour.[14] The scholastics had a definite idea of proper conduct which passed into mainstream European culture as 'courtesy'. As with the word taste, courtesy's cognates in all European tongues have the same meaning: *courtoisie* in French, *cortesia* in Italian and *Hubescheit* in German all signify exactly the same thing. Etymologically, this is 'how people behave at court'.

Manners became a means of objectifying certain taboos and giving expression to the self-image of an emerging bourgeoisie: middle-class, consuming town-dwellers. In exactly the way that the concept of taste was to evolve into a code for accepted gentility, manners became more and more refined so that they no longer meant general conduct, but signified a certain caste's idea of acceptable etiquette. This interpretation of behaviour is not necessarily normal.

We respect cleanliness and order in the social consumption of food but in his *Origin of Table Manners* (1978) Claude Lévi-Strauss observed that respect for eating quietly is a modern European phenomenon. He discovered that the table manners of 'primitive' people (he was thinking of the South American Indians) were not so much the crude fumblings of 'primitives' as an adjustable code which could be used as a language to communicate different moods and ideas. Eating habits are not innocent behaviour, but a method of broadcasting attitudes; some methods are vilified, others approved. As late as the nineteenth century the French maintained the Spanish custom (alive still in Arabia) of belching after a satisfactory

Medieval Table Manners

A number of people gnaw a bone and then put it back in the dish – this is a serious offense.

A man who clears his throat when he eats and one who blows his nose in the tablecloth are both ill-bred.

If a man wipes his nose on his hand at table because he knows no better, then he is a fool.

If a man snorts like a seal when he eats, as some people do, and smacks his chops like a Bavarian yokel, he has given up all good breeding.

Do not scrape your throat with your bare hand while eating; but if you have to, do it politely with your coat.

It is not decent to poke your fingers into your ears or eyes, as some people do, or to pick your nose while eating. These three habits are bad.

Adapted from Tannhauser's *Hofzucht* by Norbert Elias in *The Civilising Process*, 1939

Above Baldassare Castiglione, seen here in a portrait by Raphael, wrote *Il libro del cortegiano* (*The Book of the Courtier*). An influential attempt to codify manners, this is the source of many of our ideas about gentlemanly behaviour.

Right above The increasing number of books about behaviour and physiognomy appearing in the late eighteenth century demonstrates a growing inclination towards scientific analysis of character and appearance.

Right below Squeamishness about vocabulary – note the breast/bosom distinction in this caricature – was sure evidence of an emergent middle-class, uncertain about their language and tastes.

meal to demonstrate a favourable repleteness. Since the Renaissance eating habits have been acknowledged as a form of non-verbal language.[15]

Table manners demonstrate what Lévi-Strauss called a 'compulsory message'. Cutlery is just one means of moderating our relationship with the external world. In medieval Europe it was customary to eat out of a common dish. Crucially, for fastidious Westerners, cutlery achieves a distance between self and object. In non-Western cultures, eating implements are intended to preserve the food from the malign influence of the eater. In the West the same implements are regarded as a means of maintaining internal purity and external grace. Health (so-called) is only the latest of an endless line of fads which have dominated European behaviour at table: wine was once denied to children not on grounds of well-being, but because their virulent young spirits might improperly acquire its potency. Health is itself a matter of taste.

Since Baldassare Castiglione's *Il libro del cortegiano* (1528), the first modern book of manners, there has been an element in Western thought which places appearance above feeling. Castiglione's book was full of ideas which marked the beginning of the process, studied here, of interpreting artefacts in terms of behaviour. Castiglione's *sprezzatura* was the first expression of taste in everyday behaviour. A contrived, clever, courtly manner, its very artificiality put it at odds with nature. It was, by definition, artificial.

This form of self-awareness was a modern awakening. Establishing the standards for proper courtly behaviour was a way of

CHARACTERS from NATURE

Roland Barthes, a prince of distinctions. The great French *philosophe*, initially dedicated to shining the light of critical reason into the murk of the everyday meaning of things, became increasingly obscure as his career progressed. He was run over by a laundry truck in Paris in 1980.

structuring the world. From that moment behaviour was understood in terms of good and bad. But while courtiers, philosophers and anthropologists understand art and gestures, they are less certain about how objects and images communicate meaning. Cesare Lombroso, Professor of Psychiatry and Forensic Medicine at Turin (dedicatee of Max Nordau's notorious *Entartung*), took the eighteenth-century idea that beauty has a moral character to an extreme in his attempt to typify criminal types by their distinguishing features, but he was predicting a sort of pseudo-science that the Second World War was to discredit.

In post-war Paris there was a different mood of intellectual speculation. Roland Barthes, Professor at the Ecole Normale des Hautes Etudes, knew his audience: it was a sophisticated one for whom reading was already a nearly sacred rite. French intellectuals of the 1950s were already familiar with Marx, Freud, their own native theatre of the absurd, their own new wave films, the new novel, as well as pre-war surrealism. With the ground prepared in this way, acceptance of Barthes's structural analysis was considerably easier than it would have been in England or the United States. Like the other 'new' critics, he was chiefly concerned with literature and language, but, inevitably, his close reading of texts spilt over into close readings of objects. For so athletic an intellectual, it was but a short leap from, say, a stylistic analysis of Flaubert to a structural analysis of the new Citroën, steak and chips, or detergent.

Paradoxically, despite his dedication to explication, Barthes's successive critical works get more and more obscure. In his early collection of essays, *Mythologies* (1957), he writes in an unscientific, lapidary and brilliantly terse and ironic manner. There is a witty revelation on each page. The latter and far more detailed *Système de la Mode* (1967) is perhaps his most powerful and most baffling work. Wit is replaced by algorithms and organograms. He looks at fashion as presented in magazines as a system, a structure in its own right. Fashion is an identifiable set of signs by which society communicates its concerns. Thus Roland Barthes, in his search for interpreted meaning in everyday things, was to the catwalks of Paris 4ème what Lévi-Strauss was to the Polynesians.

Umberto Eco, Professor of Philosophy at Bologna University, has been more successful than Barthes in applying high-falutin literary theory to the everyday world. Eco has been accused of 'intellectual slumming', just as Roland Barthes might have been accused of 'haute vulgarization' in writing about Marilyn Monroe in the same sentence as the Académie Française. Eco defended his assault on the modern world in this way:

> Today in Pompeii tourists are visiting murals depicting Romans with huge penises; originally meant as adverts for brothels, they are now considered great art. In the eighteenth century Telemann was thought a greater composer than Bach; in the nineteenth, Eugene Sue a greater writer than Balzac. In 200 years we may consider Picasso inferior to the man currently responsible for the Coca-Cola commercials . . . So we should never be afraid to analyse marginal or inferior manifestations of our culture.[16]

Our views on the character of the world itself are equally vulnerable, and our respect for nature and individual countries has varied in the course of time.

In pre-industrial, let alone pre-electronic, ages, nature was not necessarily benign. In medieval chronicles nature is often presented as hostile and menacing. Mountains, quite properly, were once regarded as fearsome. The concept of the sublime in landscape was, as life imitates art, largely influenced by the paintings of Salvator Rosa and developed by Mrs Radcliffe in her bravura accounts of the Appenines. Turner's better Italian pictures capture something of the vastness of the mood. It is significant that a love of nature was accommodated into culture at just the moment when industrial urban expansion threatened it. In this sense the entire Romantic movement was remedial. Sir Uvedale Price and Richard Payne Knight, neighbours in Herefordshire as well as in spirit, and authors of, respectively, *Essays on the Picturesque* and *The Landscape* (both 1794), were among the most important influences on the English picturesque movement – that sensibility which defined itself as art imitating nature and became refined into nature imitating art.

It was an astonishing episode in the history of taste. Price and Knight believed that material things have certain qualities which render them, say, beautiful, sublime or picturesque. Following Edmund Burke, who argued in his *Treatise on the Sublime and the Beautiful* (1765) that beautiful things have a capacity to relax the nerves, Price contented himself with enumerating the things that contained those relaxing qualities in the highest degree. Price clearly assumed that humankind had a particu-

lar sense attuned to perceive these qualities – an apprehension dismissed by William Thomson in his *Enquiry into the Elementary Principles of Taste* (1768): 'there are almost as many different opinions concerning taste, as there are persons who lay claim to it'. While most eighteenth-century debate on the subject was conducted in these long, slow rallies, as if by accident, Price codified the rules which define and therefore limit our expectations of the English landscape, and which are still with us today.

Just as our relationship with nature is not fixed and determined, one country's attitude to another – now amused, now disinterested, now scornful – reflects changing taste as surely as the fluctuating reputations of great artists.

The British reaction to Italy provides one of the most engaging and revealing examples. Few things seem more evocatively Victorian than the figure of Punch, but Mr Punch, whose features betray it, was originally Pulcinella of the Neapolitan *commedia dell'arte* of 1600. He only acquired his English wife, Judy, in 1818 at the end of a progressive – and unrequited – infatuation of one country for the other.

So complete was the English absorption of Italian architecture, marbles and paintings that when travelling through Italy in 1786–8 Goethe wished he had a 'cultured Englishman' as a companion. Italy was an idea as much as a country, so much so that, despite a generalized assumption among English travellers that Italians were popish, not to be trusted, idle and lascivious, their home country was held in very particular regard for centuries.

A transition occurred in the late eighteenth century, when milordly amateurism sickened

Left above   'Nature', which is presently regarded as benign and benificent, at least when it takes the form of 'unspoilt' landscape, was once, as in this picture by Salvator Rosa, considered hostile and fearful.

Left below   Evolving technical developments allowed man to put nature in its place by packaging it for aesthetic consumption. The English landscape, as pioneered by Richard Payne Knight, is not 'natural' but an artful confection.

So apparently 'English', Punch is derived from the Italian *commedia dell'arte*.

into scholarship. Between William Roscoe's *Life of Lorenzo de' Medici* (1795) and J. A. Symonds's *Renaissance in Italy* (1875) there was an explosion of popular books about Italian life, history and culture. Of these books, spontaneous, impressionistic, unscholarly, Charles Dickens's *Pictures from Italy* (1846) was perhaps the best written, if the least influential. F. T. Palgrave's edition of Murray's *Handbook for Travellers in Italy* (1843) was instrumental in changing British taste. Later, the guide book was taken in two different directions: one by John Ruskin, the other by Augustus Hare. Born in Rome, Hare wrote several guide books to Italy and had a natural mother called Italima. These personal details are all witness to the cult of things Italian, which extended to religion and Romanticism. John Henry Newman, an Anglican clergyman, visited Rome in 1833; he left it well on the way to becoming a Catholic. Dismayed and enthralled by the Eternal City, he wrote: 'The first thought one has of the place is awful – that you see the great enemy of God . . . Next, when you enter the museums, galleries and libraries, a fresh world is opened to you – that of imagination and taste.'

Romanticism, the first democratic, mass-media movement in art, depending for its force on a combination of word and image, which in a sense provides the scriptural origins of pop culture, tended to popularize travel. Byron got his first impressions of Italy second-hand. Of Venice he wrote,

Otway, Radcliffe, Schiller, Shakespeare's art
Had stamped her image in me.

In poetry Wordsworth, Keats, Shelley, Coleridge and Browning monopolized Italian subjects. In prose it was Edward Bulwer Lytton and George Eliot. Roscoe's *The Life of Lorenzo de' Medici* (1795) was a source for Pre-Raphaelitism, but in a curious way the Pre-Raphaelite Brotherhood rejected Italian subject matter, just as their spiritual forebears, the Nazarenes, had begun to create in Rome from 1809 a style of painting that was entirely German. Thomas Stothard, who drew the figures for the engraved illustrations of Samuel Rogers's influential *Italy* (1830), had never actually been there; a synthetic stereotype was passed on to an entire generation. Although Holman Hunt, Millais and Rossetti had been inspired by engravings[17] of the Pisan Campo Santo when they founded the Brotherhood in

1848, they were all without direct experience of Italy and its art. Holman Hunt explained their reluctance to acquire it: 'In these days men of British blood . . . should not subject themselves to the influence of masters alien to the sentiments of the great English poets and thinkers.'

In 1849 Hunt exhibited a painting based on and accompanied by a long quotation from Edward Bulwer Lytton's *Rienzi* (published in 1835 and dedicated to Alessandro Manzoni, author of *I promessi sposi*). Rienzi is shown as the patriotic liberator of Rome. But contemporary Italian painting had no influence on mid-nineteenth-century British art. The Pre-Raphaelite Brotherhood was only one of a number of attempts to capture the purity of earlier Italian art, sometimes through the example of contemporary second-rate English literature. The rehabilitation of Botticelli, which preceded that of El Greco, was typical, as was Alfred Stevens's designs for the proposed new bronze doors of the Geological Museum in Jermyn Street (1846–9), an exercise in higher pastiche.

Another example of a cultish vogue for things Italian was the brief fashion for the Garibaldi blouse, a version of Giuseppe Garibaldi's famous red shirts (which were in fact supplied to him by Thresher and Glenny of the Strand as part of London's contribution to the Sicilian expedition of 1860). The Italian liberator also became a popular model for Staffordshire figures, and a biscuit, still in production today, was named after him.

Inspired by the magnificent example of past Italian art, Sir Joseph Noel Paton – a painter whose *Dream of Michelangelo* (late 1840s) is in the William Morris Gallery, Walthamstow, London – wrote, in an era of copious mediocrity, an outstandingly bad poem:

No, Buonarroti, thou shalt not subdue
My mind with thy Thor-hammer! All that play
Of ponderous science with Titanic thew
And spastic tendon – marvellous, 'tis true –
Says nothing to my soul

The quality of Paton's verse is perhaps appropriate to a taste that went into decline almost as soon as it had finished its ascent. Two such unlikely bedfellows as Karl Marx and Queen Victoria both condemned the Garibaldi cult. The communist dubbed it 'a miserable spectacle of imbecility', while the monarch found herself 'half ashamed of being the head of a nation capable of such follies' (although she did have an Italianate villa called Osborne built for herself on the Isle of Wight). What Byron called Italy's 'fatal gift of beauty' could lead to dismay, and the taste for things Italian became less robust. Browning's lugubrious line, 'What was left, I wonder, when the kissing had to stop?' hints at a mood of disfavour.

Exposure to Italian music was an inescapable fact of life in Victorian Britain. Grand opera, maudlin songs for an accompanied pianoforte, and the itinerant organ grinder offered each of the British social classes vicarious contact with Italian culture. But as early as the 1840s the popularity of Rossini, Donizetti and Bellini was being challenged by the Germans Mendelssohn and Weber. By the time W. B. Scott paid his last visit to Italy in 1873, he found that Italy helped 'decrease my love of painting' and added, 'How does the traveller begin to loathe the Madonna.' In Britain Italian

music was kept alive not so much by composers as by singers and instrumentalists and impresarios (itself an Italian word). This change in status has contributed to the prejudice, still not entirely eradicated, that Italians are amiable buffoons. There is a hint of this in Mrs Beeton's *Household Management* (1861) which declares that 'With the exception of macaroni, [Italians] have no specially characteristic article of food.'

Improved communications were a fundamental influence in turning English taste away from Italy. Familiarity breeds contempt, so for as long as Italy was impossibly remote, artists were happy to provide imaginative confections of Italian scenery and the public was happy to be beguiled by them. Whereas in 1820 John Keats took four and a half weeks to sail from Gravesend to Naples, and in 1833 the painter Charles West Cope (whose picture *Italian Hostelry* – in fact painted in London in 1836 – hangs in Liverpool's Walker art gallery) took more than seven days and nights to travel by road from Paris to Milan, by the 1860s the railway had reduced the London–Milan journey to a mere fifty hours.

Mrs Beeton's amused dismay passes straight through to Norman Douglas, although in his case the subject is treated with more exuberance, charity and knowledge than Mrs Beeton could muster. In *Old Calabria* (1919) Douglas revels in curious details: Venose displayed 'a reposeful dirtiness, not vulgar and chaotic, but testifying to time-honoured neglect, to a feudal contempt of cleanliness'; 'one old man . . . was wont habitually to engulph twenty-two litres of wine a day'; 'mice . . . are cooked into a paste and given to children'.

While there is some mockery in Douglas's account of pre-industrial Italy, there is also an element of *et in Arcadia ego*, which was to be expressed in a new, romantic interpretation of Italy and the Mediterranean stimulated by the privations of the Second World War.

Norman Douglas's ghost stalks the pages of the marvellous cookery books written by Elizabeth David. By the time Mrs David's *Italian Food* appeared in 1954, Italy was overdue for a revival. In her introduction to successive editions Mrs David repeatedly invokes authenticity. The subtext of her descriptions of England in the 1950s is a critique of English life and manners at least as important as that of the more loudly trumpeted contemporary Angry Young Men. Being concerned with sentiment as much as with recipes, the popularity of Mrs David's books proved the centrality of taste to the modern consumer.

Born to shop

The meaning of taste in history has swooped and veered between physical sensation and aesthetic predilection. Wordsworth was worried that a taste for poetry might be confused with something so indifferent as a taste for rope-dancing or for sherry.[18] The same can be said of the Italian word *gusto* or of the French *goût* and the German *Geschmack*. It is a concept at once substantial and suggestive, the metaphorical transfer from passive sensations to intellectual acts of discrimination. Taste with a capital T developed from an abstraction to an attribute. As Raymond Williams noted in *Keywords* (1976), 'We have only to think of related sense words, such as touch or feel in their extended and metaphorical usages, which

Elizabeth David's cookery books changed the British palate and the British appetite. A neo-romantic reaction to the dreary post-war days, Mrs David's lascivious recipes were perfectly expressed in John Minton's illustrations.

Johann Winckelmanns,
Präsidentens der Alterthümer zu Rom, und Scrittore der Vaticanischen Bibliothek,
Mitglieds der Königl. Englischen Societät der Alterthümer zu London, der Maleracademie
von St. Luca zu Rom, und der Hetrurischen zu Cortona,

Geschichte der Kunst
des Alterthums.

Erster Theil.

Mit Königl. Pohlnisch- und Churfürstl. Sächs. allergnädigsten Privilegio.

Dresden, 1764.
In der Waltherischen Hof-Buchhandlung.

have not been abstracted, capitalized and in such ways regulated, to realize the essential distinction.'

In 1755 Johann Joachim Winckelmann, a librarian from Dresden, went to live in the Roman palace of Cardinal Albani, taking with him a bag full of rationalist philosophy. He was appointed Prefect of Roman Antiquities in 1763, and his early distinction between Greek and Roman marbles laid the basis for modern archaeology. He also laid the scholarly basis for neo-classicism, a taste in art, architecture and design that became – in an age on the verge of mass production – perhaps the first consumer cult.

Winckelmann found in Greek art a confirmation of his personal theory of beauty. He considered that simplicity, harmony, functionalism (in both structure and adaptation to the local environment) and respect for materials were all prerequisites for the achievement of beauty in architectural design. He did not see that either colour or ornament had any part to play in it. Beauty resulted from a certain arrangement of shapes and forms which were in some way expressive of the ideal. This was what he meant by his demand for 'noble simplicity'.

In providing a theoretical basis for the neo-classical aesthetic Winckelmann was a profound, if esoteric, influence on the history of European and American taste. A contemporary of his, Jeanne Antoinette Poisson, had a more immediate contribution to make to the newly developing European material culture. Known to history as Madame de Pompadour, Mademoiselle Poisson's astonishing career demonstrated the close relationship between social aspiration and modern taste – a relationship which has been more or less inseparable ever since. Pompadour made tangible the elevated idea of 'taste'. It ceased to be metaphorical, and became instead a particular vision of haut-bourgeois style. She turned *arriviste* middle-class snobbery into a minor movement in the history of art, creating 'positional' goods two centuries before the term was invented. Hers was the '*objet du goût*', her legacy the discretionary part of the market-place, where all modern consumers are adrift between the Scylla of conformity and the Charybdis of error. Madame de Pompadour was the inventor of the consumer product.

Ever the one for the grand gesture, the ambitious young Poisson was pleased to drive, as circumstances demanded, either a pink or a blue phaeton across the path of Louis XV as he hunted or pursued his botanical interests in the forests around Paris. With style, she wore pink in the blue phaeton, and blue in the pink one. The gesture did not go unnoticed by the monarch, who, bored with the queen, had also recently lost his mistress. He picked her up at a fancy-dress ball held at Versailles in 1744. Apparently without irony, Poisson went as Diana the Hunter. She easily captivated the king with her wit and coruscating conversation, her singing, dancing and musicianship.

He gave her an estate at Pompadour and the title of marquise. She gave him everything except her body, an exercise in restraint that in the era before Freud was not properly understood, but which throws into dizzying confusion her willingness to pose enticingly and fleshily in the nude for François Boucher's voluptuous *Toilet of Venus* (1751, once in the

Above   Madame de Pompadour invented the '*objet du goût*', the first conscious expression of the consumer mentality.

Left   Johann Joachim Winckelmann, who pioneered scholarly study of classical antiquity and laid the intellectual base of neo-classical taste.

collection of the Vicomte de la Béraudière). Her nude portrait, while not without a strong erotic *frisson*, was intended for her own apartments at Versailles, not for the titillation of the king. It is an image designed to confer status, in this case divine, on the sitter. The once humble Poisson had a high regard for her own worth. At court she became notorious because, with true middle-class snobbery, she conducted herself with chilling hauteur.

Jules Beaujoint published this ditty in his *Secret Memoirs of Madame la Marquise de Pompadour* (1885):

> The Birth of Jesus made,
> At court a stir indeed,
> And Louis in a coach drove off
> To Pompadour with speed.
> Said he, 'The Child we'll go and see',
> Said she, 'No, not at all;
> They'd better bring the Child to me,
> I never make a call.'

Madame de Pompadour posed for Boucher's *Toilet of Venus*.

Madame de Pompadour's exercise of taste was facilitated by ready access to money and is thus a prototype for modern consumerism: it is often said that her collection was the most remarkable assemblage of possessions ever acquired by a French citizen. While Louis XV had the greatest difficulty in getting between her legs, she slid easily in and out of his bank account. Nancy Mitford's *Madame de Pompadour* (1954), based on sources that include de Hausset, Croy, Bernis, Luynes and Maurette, has her saying, 'He doesn't mind signing for a million, but hates to part with little sums out of his purse.'

She bought house after house to decorate for the king: Crécy near Dreux; Montretout at Saint-Cloud and La Celle nearby; others at Compiègne and Fontainebleau. She filled the Hermitage at Versailles with fresh flowers every day. She had the architect Lassurance design a house called Bellevue near Sèvres (which had scented china flowers from Vincennes), and Les Réservoirs at Versailles. Her Parisian house, the Hôtel d'Evreux, is now known as the Elysée Palace, a legacy that has had incalculable esoteric influence on the taste of French presidents.

Madame de Pompadour was the *ancien régime* version of the 'born to shop' phenomenon. Her pursuit of material acquisitions was on the sinister side of neurotic. They included Dresden, Meissen, pot-pourris from Chantilly, sculptures, carvings and ornaments by Pigalle, Verberckt and Falconet, pictures by Chardin, Van Loo and, of course, François Boucher.

A Louis XV commode. French eighteenth-century furniture has been a touchstone in the history of taste.

That the measure of exquisite good taste, wherever *arrivistes* gather, is even today expressed in terms of eighteenth-century French art, architecture and design says much about the influence of Madame de Pompadour, creator of the Hôtel d'Evreux, among many other palaces.

There were also storehouses filled with other pictures, porcelain (2,000 pieces of Sèvres), tapestries, linen, tools, carriages, wine and autograph furniture (including an escritoire by J.-F. Oeben, now in the Jack and Belle Linsky Collection of the Metropolitan Museum of Art. At the Rothschilds' Waddesdon Manor in Buckinghamshire there is a gold and porcelain snuffbox with portraits of her dogs, Inès and Mimi, painted on the lid – another example of how the Pompadour *arriviste* taste crosses generations.

Although, according to Jules Beaujoint, 'the Marquise was not a blue-stocking', she left a library of 3,826 books covering such subjects as commerce, finance, industry, philosophy, theology and history. Pompadour – whom Beaujoint describes as a woman of 'severe taste' – was artistic dictator of France in the years before the Revolution: she had Jacques-Ange Gabriel design the Petit Trianon, the perfect proportions of which were later to inspire Le Corbusier in his belief that all fine architecture is the product of an invisible grid, *traces régulateurs*. She also created the Cabinets du Roi at Versailles, and, with her intuitive flair for dealing with craftsmen and designers, arranged the Gobelin tapestries, the damasks, the secretaires, the bibelots and the pictures. Perhaps as a consequence of her preferred diet of vanilla, truffles and celery, Pompadour, France's first arbiter of taste, died at the age of forty-two.

The story of Madame de Pompadour, with its engaging details, is not of mere anecdotal interest. Her extraordinary position as artist of the state gave her huge power and influence to indulge her aesthetic preferences. Her canvas was not stapled to a stretcher, but covered all of modern material France. Her achievements created the role of 'taste-maker', whose ghost exists today, but her understanding of marginal utility and the role of desire in design led to the '*objet du goût*' which has passed, by a route described elsewhere in this book, from mistresses of kings to owners of chain stores.

In Britain less elevated bourgeois taste at the time of Pompadour was represented by furniture, ceramics and the idea of the *souvenir*. Popular design was already in the market-place in the late eighteenth century. Neo-classicism expressed this taste sometimes uncertainly. Josiah Wedgwood and his artist John Flaxman extended trade far beyond Joshua Reynolds's conception of the world, converting a peasant craft into an industrial business supported by the ancestor of the modern skill of marketing. He gave class to the primitive kilns of Staffordshire and became a major influence on the development of taste.

Wedgwood's creamware service was inspired by the chaste simplicity, noted also by Winckelmann, of antique art (although in fact antecedents of Wedgwood were doing much the same thing in Rome). However, this was not just an aesthetic preference; from the mass-producer's point of view there were practical and economic imperatives for this desired simplicity in that simple designs were easier to make than the more elaborate rococo ones.

In furniture there was a desire to achieve certain standards of dignity and order. The Preface to George Hepplewhite's *The Cabinet-Maker and Upholsterer's Guide* (1794), a compilation of designs for jobbing craftsmen to copy and for the gentleman pleasurably to

survey, declares, 'To unite elegance and utility, and blend the useful with the agreeable, has ever been considered a difficult, but an honourable task.'

Hepplewhite's designs were described as 'good and proper', an interesting phrase that hints at the relevance of manners and appropriateness to English taste. The *Guide*, besides being a hymn to gentility, reveals itself as a confident arbiter of taste: 'Mahogany chairs have seats of horse hair, plain, striped, chequered &c. at pleasure . . . Japanned chairs should always have linen or cotton cushions.' Hepplewhite's designs were so adaptable and so durable and successful that they have been continuously reproduced, but it was not until the mid-nineteenth century that a technical

A teapot for eternity. Josiah Wedgwood was inspired by what he imagined was the chaste simplicity of antique art. Eighty years later archaeology proved that classical buildings had been garishly decorated. The eighteenth-century conception of 'antique' was a projection on to the past of contemporary taste.

revolution in furniture manufacture radicalized taste.

Innovations in ceramics came sooner. Interestingly, improvements in the processes of making ceramics, in the brave Wedgwood tradition, coincided with an emerging neo-classical taste – the artificial stone produced at Coade's factory in Lambeth helped to make the neo-classical version of the antique popularly accessible. Since the collection of classical statues at Fontainebleau had become famous, they had served as marks of modernity, as Montesquieu explained in his *Voyage d'Italie*: 'These statues cannot be sufficiently looked at, for it is from them that the Moderns have built up their systems of proportions.' There was an element of élitism, even snobbery of the intellectual sort, in possessing such a canon.

By about 1700, foreign craftsmen in Rome were preparing lead reproductions of ancient statues for commercial manufacture, for those who could afford neither original antiques nor the more costly bronze copies. While Wedgwood was not above making heads of ancient worthies as souvenirs, the real popularization of antique imagery and ideals came from Mrs Coade and from John Cheere's sculpture yards at Hyde Park Corner, illustrated as the frontispiece of William Hogarth's *Analysis of Beauty* (1756), itself an examplar of modern taste in the arts. With Josiah Wedgwood, John Cheere (1709–87) was the first Englishman to realize the potential market for tokens of taste. By collecting Cheere's mass-produced souvenirs, anyone could have a collection of marbles as ennobling as François I's.

By the mid-nineteenth century, such didacticism was institutionalized. In Paris a Musée des Copies was established by Thiers and in London in 1864 Brucciani opened a 2,500-ft gallery of plaster casts in Russell Street, Covent Garden, portentously called a 'Galleria delle Belle Arti'. Brucciani's statues were not only educative (in that they prepared visitors for their trips to Florence, Naples and Rome); they also found their way into all the provincial art schools of Britain, as required since 1859 by the Lords of the Committee of Education of the Privy Council. In a prototype gesture of suburban disdain for Italy, *The Art Journal* reasoned that the success of Brucciani's collection lay in the fact that Covent Garden provided an environment 'much purer' and therefore more conducive to contemplation than Italy. At the same time, when certain casts found their way into private hands, status was conferred on the owner. This form of intellectual property was highly valued. Contemporary garden statuary is a mongrel descendant of these copies.

The development of taste as an idea and as an aesthetic prescription parallels the rise in popular expectations which grew with the increase in spending power. Taste and money are inseparable in nineteenth-century culture. Honoré de Balzac was obsessive about money (even while he romantically despised the monied classes); his descriptions of interiors created by financiers and industrialists betray the dependence this generation of consumers had on the antique in forming and projecting their taste.

The term 'consumer' had come into use as a description of bourgeois economic activity in the eighteenth century. In the new markets of the rapidly industrializing nations, making and using became known as producing and consuming. It is interesting to chart the relative decline of the old-fashioned, more genteel word 'customer' against the rise of the more abstract, aggressive 'consumer'. Semantically, 'customer' suggests familiarity and regularity and a one-to-one relationship with a retailer or a manufacturer, while the remote 'consumer' is a more relevant, impersonal tag in global markets giddy with excess. 'Consume' almost always has an unfavourable, even hostile, connotation, as in 'consumed by fire'. Tuberculosis was known as consumption during the whole period when it was a killer disease, and Vance Packard's *The Hidden Persuaders* (1956) makes great play with the derogatory term 'consumer society'.

The history of the word 'consumer' reveals the development of the Western economy. Mass production and all that it entails – investment, long lead-times, low unit costs and ready availability – replaced a system where simple makers could articulate and satisfy needs; the new distant customers alienated from the production process became consumers. Deconstructing meanings in this way helps explain how taste operates in the modern world. Just as the modern idea of money involves credit (from the Latin *credo*, I believe, or I trust), the concept of taste came to fill the vacuum created by the possibility of limitless consumption brought about by the possibility of limitless credit. The etymology of credit makes it clear that money, like taste, is very much an act of faith.

The Frankfurt School social scientists Walter Benjamin and Theodor Adorno noted the extraordinary paradox that under capitalism taste is not autonomous – as one might expect in a system which promotes competitive individualism – but tends to be collective. Market researchers know what are the most effective contemporary symbols of privilege and instruments of status.

The status symbol is as significant today as it was in Madame de Pompadour's time, but it takes different forms and serves different purposes. It is not surprising that in the eighteenth century tokens of taste were classical statuary and in the nineteenth moral values. In a century still cowed by the machine, consumer durables have become touchstones of value, and none is no numinous as the wrist-watch. Its very familiarity and availability has, by a Darwinian process, forced special and intricate patterns of discrimination on consumers. What Antinous was to Cardinal Albani, the expensive wrist-watch is to the taste-makers of the late twentieth century. Giovanni Agnelli of Fiat has a personal foible: he wears his on the outside of his cuff.

Although not the most expensive, the most exceptional watch as status symbol is the Swiss Rolex, since its reputation is based on technical merit (a patent for its remarkable watertight stem was granted in 1926). This gave rise to an aura of professionalism and expertise which has since proved especially attractive. Ever since Mercedes Gleitze wore a Rolex Oyster for a heavily publicized cross-Channel swim in 1927, Rolex has been more than merely a watch.

Before the First World War wrist-watches, as compared to fob-watches, were considered effeminate, but when artillerymen needed the convenience of a wrist-watch (as bicyclists had

The wrist-watch provides even men of conservative tastes with an opportunity to express personality. Giovanni Agnelli (*above*) always wears his wrist-watch *over* his cuff.

Right above   The classic man's watch is the Rolex. The company's advertising, featuring leading mountaineers and musicians, has stressed the development of the individual as much as the product, turning the watch into powerful shorthand.

Right below   The Cartier 'Tank' watch was evolved during the First World War, when soldiers began to wear wrist-watches. Its military nomenclature helped create a new market.

just before them), they became important symbols. Ever since, the basic architecture of the wrist-watch has depended on innovations made for the trenches. The number of press advertisements for new bracelets coming on to the market between 1914 and 1918 attests to its growing popularity, even though conservative spokesmen for the watch industry thought it was an idiotic fashion to expose so sensitive a mechanism on the most restless part of the body.

Because of the stigma of effeminacy, the wrist-watch has always been marketed in a pointedly masculine way. Cartier's most famous wrist-watches are the 'Tank' (made for the US Army Tank Corps, another innovation of the First World War) and the 'Santos' named after the swashbuckling pioneer aviator Santos Du Mont), while all Rolex models make some sort of persuasive appeal to professionalism – that of the diver, the aviator, the racing-car driver or the opera singer.

Ever since the 1920s Rolex has concerned itself with developing its customers as much as its watches, and for fifteen years the simple theme has been 'famous people wear Rolexes'. These people include Yehudi Menuhin, Kiri Te Kanawa and Reinhold Messner. An article in *Campaign* (November 1987) explored reactions to 'the timeless timepiece'. Dave Trott, socialist Buddhist partner in the advertising agency Gold Greenlees Trott, commented: 'I wouldn't be seen dead in one. What it says is that you have no originality and you need to wear an accepted badge to say you have made money. It's like people used to wear clothes and shoes with the YSL label on the outside, or buy a Porsche 911 and never drive outside

Soho. It's a cliché.' But rival ad agency boss John Hegarty more shrewdly retorted: 'It says I've made it. I've achieved that, done it, sorted that area out. It is about two things: awareness and achievement. It is also obvious with a Rolex that you have money because they cost so much.'

The same was once said of the Apollo Belvedere. But unlike Apollo, Montres Rolex SA know that sales go up when they increase the price: as Andre Heiniger explained, 'We are in the luxury business. We are selling taste, selling fashion, selling status. If you have a Rolex you are a member of a select international club.' Franco Zeffirelli considers a Rolex 'above fashion. It is standard . . . in my own work I never try to be fashionable. Never. And the same could be said for the watch I have chosen to wear.'

It is significant that Rolex users are so self-conscious about their choice of wrist-watch and that to many of them its value lies either in its overt expression of professionalism or in its reticent expression of neutrality. The proper maintenance of the middle class's self-regard depends on their values being necessarily good, superior to those of the upper as well as the lower classes. This is why snobbery is essentially a distinction of the middle classes and why the Rolex is an essentially middle-class watch.

Brixton and Vienna

Between 1850 and 1910 the population of Britain grew from 27 to 45 million. The growth was in the urban classes. When this huge, new and (by some standards) ignorant class

emerged, supply and demand was no longer controlled by the *cognoscenti*, but by the principles of market economics. This produced such a fundamental revolution in behaviour that it soon become clear that Reynolds was wrong: there was more than one taste and a great many decent people apparently did not share his.

The new middle class neither knew nor cared about Reynolds's polite strictures, but preferred to clutter themselves with meretricious junk, mass-produced by cynical manipulators of the means of production in Birmingham, Sheffield and Glasgow. A bookcase got up to look like the west front of Lincoln cathedral was typical. For the nineteenth-century consumer, the rules of taste were replaced by market forces; philosophical musings were replaced by homely tracts admonishing avaricious and fashion-crazed housewives for their want of judgement and their excess of competitive acquisitiveness.

Charles Eastlake in his *Hints on Household Taste* (1868) described with the unfluctuating certainty of someone comfortable with his prejudices the proper application of the principle of taste to all the minutiae of domestic life. He argued that the artistic chaos of most homes resulted from no one being trained to make aesthetic judgements (and in saying this he echoed the rationalism of the eighteenth century). He believed that guidance in the matter of what he called 'right taste' should form a necessary part of every genteel woman's education. His use of the absolute 'right', as opposed to the somewhat less certain 'good', reveals most clearly his conviction that one taste alone is correct. Nor is he innocent of the charge of puritanism, revealed in his abhorrence of consumerism and its appetite for novelty:

> When did people first adopt the monstrous notion that the 'last pattern out' must be the best? Is good taste so rapidly progressive that every mug which leaves the potter's hands surpasses in shape the last which he moulded? But it is feared that, instead of progressing, we have, for some ages at least, gone hopelessly backward in the art of manufacture.

This charge of shoddy workmanship levelled at the workshop of the world was a powerful weapon in the aesthetician's armoury. It is true that applied ornament was often used to camouflage manufacturing faults, but in his criticism of popular decoration Eastlake became confused about taste and design:

> This commonplace taste . . . compels us to rest on chairs and to sit at tables which are designed in accordance with the worst principles of construction and invested with shapes confessedly unpicturesque. It sends us metalwork from Birmingham which is as vulgar in form as it is flimsy in execution. It decorates the finest modern porcelain with the most objectionable character of ornament.

In his strictures Eastlake may have been influenced by Augustus Pugin, visionary architect of the Gothic Revival, who made the same point, more forcibly, in his *Apology for the Revival of Christian Architecture* (1843):

> It is impossible to enumerate half the

absurdities of modern metalworkers; but all these proceed from the false notion of disguising instead of beautifying articles of utility. How many objects of ordinary use are rendered monstrous and ridiculous, simply because the artist, instead of seeking the most convenient form and then decorating it, has embodied some extravagance to conceal the real purpose for which the article has been made!

The rich brew of art and morality, the roseate view of history, caught the mood of the time, and – setting a disastrous precedent for British culture – suggested that the solution to the immediate artistic, moral and social problems of England existed at the end of a long journey back to the Middle Ages. Here Pugin imagined a world of God-driven beauty and harmony, of innocent men, of organs booming basso profundo solid, spiritual goodness. There was no smog and no proletariat, only placid, satisfied peasants. Viewed from one of Gustave Doré's railway arches, it was a persuasive vision.

But beneath the apparent certainties of Victorian England lay paradoxes which are still unresolved today. There is more snobbery in one copy of the nineteenth-century middle-class journal *Punch* than in an entire run of the patrician eighteenth-century *Gentleman's Magazine*. Pride in Britain's industrial eminence was moderated by disquiet at the quality, purpose and appearance of most of what was produced. While paternalism suggests a positivist belief in progress and improvement, the aesthetic zealots sought their inspiration in distant history. The concern for the moral welfare of the working classes, though real, was also pragmatic, in that the country was more troubled by fears of public disorder and urban insurrection than popular views of the Victorian age allow. Above all, the interests of a ruling minority were contrived to appear to coincide with the good of the many.

The idea of taste has a peculiar force which nineteenth-century philanthropists were quick to exploit. Visions of depraved and enlightened taste were the invisible illustrations in self-help tracts, designed to help demoralized consumers. The paternalistic cultures of the nineteenth century set up museums to guide popular taste to more elevated (which was to say formal, antique) levels by exhibiting objects held to be of the highest artistic perfection. A necessary extension of this idea of presenting exemplars for imitation was, at least to the paternalist, the provision of equal and opposite exemplars for avoidance.

Nowhere was such philanthropy and opportunism, public purpose and self-interest, combined with more genuine enthusiasm for popularizing art than in the person and career of Sir Henry Cole (1808–82). From an unpromising training as a civil servant in the Public Record Office, Cole created a curriculum vitae to rival any; he was chillingly described as 'over active' by one of Queen Victoria's aides, and at mid-career he played a leading role in the conception and execution of one of the century's most significant cultural events: the Great Exhibition of the Industry of All Nations held in London's Hyde Park in 1851.

Cole's most influential accomplice was Prince Albert, whose interest in manufacturing ranged from export performance to the

Prince Albert invented the idea of a Great Exhibition to improve public taste. The 1851 show at the Crystal Palace in London was immensely popular. A primal media event, it suggested that the entire world was available for consumption.

viciousness of superfluous decoration (although he did himself specify tartan linoleum for Balmoral). While the aims of the exhibition organizers had been didactic, the mood of the public was celebratory. Promoted as an exercise in national pride, the underlying purpose of the Great Exhibition was to educate through exposure to the best and the worst, allowing visitors to draw their own conclusions. The intended lesson in taste may have been lost on many of the revellers, but the popular success of the enterprise encouraged Cole and his supporters to renew their educational efforts yet more energetically by other means. The profits from the Great Exhibition were used to buy some of the exhibits so as to form a permanent study collection of contemporary industrial art for public edification and enlightenment.

Cole bought 2,075 items of foreign manufacture, 1,500 goods from the East India Company and 890 from British manufacturers. In descending proportion these comprise metalwork, fabrics, enamels, furniture and ceramics. According to the *Catalogue of the Great Exhibition*, 'Each specimen has been selected for its merits in exemplifying some right principle of construction or ornament . . . to which it appeared desirable that the attention of our Students and Manufacturers should be directed.'

There were some crucial distinctions, betraying many a prejudice. Eastern products were generally illustrative of 'correct principles of ornament', but suffered from 'rude' workmanship. European specimens show 'superior skill' but are 'defective in the principles of their design'. When European products attempt direct imitation of nature, the results are 'very inferior . . . to the ruder scarfs of Tunis'. This bizarre study collection – 'illustrating the Correct principles of Taste' – was opened to the public at the Department of Practical Art's Marlborough House premises.

The gallery displaying 'The False Principles of Design' soon became known as Cole's Chamber of Horrors, a sort of industrial freak show. With true paternalistic zeal Cole produced a catalogue which listed the false principles, so visitors could be forewarned against later forays in the market-place, as opposed the museum. These false principles included: lack of symmetry, disregard of structure, formless confusion and superficial decoration. Alas,

Cole's skill with public relations did not match his flair for didactic entertainment and the Chamber of Horrors was short-lived; complaints and withdrawals by the pilloried and vilified manufacturers best versed in false principles soon made the business of organizing loans impossible rather than merely difficult.

During its short career the Chamber of Horrors attracted both public ridicule and healthy scepticism; officials found it risible, yet unsettling, but Cole had touched a nerve. His museum had to revert to the traditional idea of solemn, unquestioning contemplation of works of applied art. An astonishing experiment in setting up a public clinic where the maladies of manufacturing industry could be inspected by consumers failed, but provided a model for imitation.

Similar objections from the trades curtailed another experiment in creating a museum of bad taste in Prague. Here Gustav Pazaurek had considered showing visitors to the Northern Bohemian Museum gross and horrible things for the home, an ambition he had to forgo until he reached the more liberal province of Württemberg, where, as Director of the Industrial Museum in Stuttgart, he created his Museum of Art Indiscretions. In this he included a modern suit of armour, intended for a parvenu castle; tin boxes coloured to imitate faience; wood looking like granite; iron faked to look like Wedgwood; and 'presumptuous' metals: tin looking like silver, zinc looking like bronze. He also did not like chocolate busts of the Kaiser, proving a popular line in certain tasteless Konditoreien. Like Henry Cole, Pazaurek's aesthetic outrage was sustained by moral force: Cole damned the false, while

Bad Taste

Preciosities in material
China flower vases in the form of hollowed-
    out tree trunks
Ashtrays made of postage stamps
Senseless combinations of materials
Linoleum imitating wood or leather
Chocolate busts of the Kaiser

Faults of construction
Metal vessels for hot fluids
Unstable vases
Uncomfortable chairs
Pincushions in shape of velvet animals
Thermometers fashioned like riding whips

Brutalities of decoration
Wide margins in books
Senselessly simple bindings
Religious and patriotic motifs
Liver sausage decorated with images of
    Bismarck

Adapted from Gustav Pazaurek, *Catalogue of
the Museum of Art Indiscretions*, 1909

Pazaurek condemned anything intended to deceive the ignorant. Although one might detect the germ of modern movement ideology in the insistence of truth to materials, Pazaurek was as quick to damn the errors of undue simplicity as of undue excess.

But faults of construction were as repugnant to the Museum of Art Indiscretions as preciosities of materials. Here we find an element of functionalism creeping in: unstable vases, thermally inappropriate materials for containers, eccentric ornaments (empty shell cases and imitation helmets), thermometers fashioned like riding whips and uncomfortable chairs made out of stag's antlers were presented for obloquy. Souvenir trash, patriotic trash, religious trash and advertising trash were also included.

These were popular concerns. Henry Morley (1822–94) became a close associate of Charles Dickens, who had become acquainted with his work on reading a series called 'How to Make a Home Unhealthy' in the *Journal of Public Health*. Morley soon followed the *Zeitgeist* and switched from public health to popular taste, from the inner to the outer man. His clever parody, 'A House Full of Horrors', was published in 1852 in *Household Words*, a journal established by Dickens to monitor the growing cult of the middle-class home in the middle of the century. It was the social equivalent of the self-improving, democratic pamphlets which circulated at the same time among the new industrial workers. Morley describes the nightmares suffered by one innocent visitor to the Museum of Practical Art, a certain Mr Crumpet, as he finds himself surrounded on his return home to the new suburb of Brixton by the very objects he has been didactified into abhorring:

The matter is this: I have acquired some Correct Principles of Taste. Five weeks ago I went to the Department of Practical Art in Marlborough House to look over the museum of ornamental art. I had heard of a Chamber of Horrors there established, and I found it, and went through it with my catalogue. It was a gloomy chamber, hung round with frightful objects in curtains, carpets, clothes, lamps and what not. In each case the catalogue told me why such and such a thing wasn't endurable.

In particular:

That tray with a bit of Landseer's pictures on it, you will find to correspond with the seventy-ninth item in the Catalogue of Horrors, at which you will find these following observations. It is 'An example of popular but vulgar taste, of a low character, presenting numerous features which the student should carefully avoid: First, the centre is the piracy of the picture; Second, the picture on which most labour has been bestowed is thrown away . . . It is wrong to hide a picture by putting a teapot on it.

Mr Crumpet becomes dismayed to discover that he is actually wearing some of the unendurable clothing on show. From then on his newly acquired sensitivity in matters of taste has alarming consequences:

After hanging up my hat in the hall, I had great trouble in straightening my hair as I went into the ladies, it would stand upright at the horror of my friend's hall-paper. I had seen it in the Chamber of Horrors — perspective representations of a railway station frequently repeated. Why is it that people do not understand what I have understood quite well for the last five weeks; that pictures of any kind, and above all, perspectives, are unusually out of place repeated around a wall . . . When a picture is repeated up and down and round about the place, the result is a nightmare.

Morley gently concludes that while Cole's medicine was worth taking, a smaller dose might have been advisable. Mildly ridiculous even in its own day, Cole's prescriptions would be unthinkable now. With the passing of extrovert paternalism went behaviour so lacking in irony or in the supposed objectivity of intellectual reasoning. It was an exercise only possible in an age whose executives were backed by mighty moral certainties.

Henry Cole has provided prototypes for many things, from the professional civil servant to the Victoria and Albert Museum, but perhaps most significant of all is his role model for the embattled middle-class aesthete, outraged by the impropriety and pretension of lesser folk, dismayed by the obdurate philistinism of those of higher rank. Good taste was what made Henry Cole feel good and less threatened. Bad taste was the other thing.

Cole's use of the museum as an active medium (rather than a passive collection) was not unique. In the United States Mellon, Frick and other *nouveaux riches* were establishing, at the last historical moment when such a thing was possible, their own private collections rivalling in splendour and swagger the national collections of Europe. Their presence, both physical and spiritual, gave the public certain expectations of art – and still does. What animus drove the collectors? The answer is this: an art collection validates the status and confirms the arrival of the parvenu.[19] The Firestone heiress said her compulsion to collect eighteenth-century furniture was similar to the effect peanuts had on her: have one and you want the whole lot.

Museums buttressed self-made egos and gave to emergent nations the sanction of the past. They stabilized art, but art needs to be volatile, so to redress the stability of the marble halls, the concept of the avant-garde emerged. The avant-garde (which, at least semantically, has military and then political origins) is fundamental to an understanding of modern taste. Somewhere out there is a huge graveyard of French expressions, memorials to past conceits and fancies which died when France ceased to dominate global culture. Avant-garde belongs alongside *thé dansant* and *noblesse oblige*; it comes from a period when culture was a battlefield, when creativity could be quantified by capitalizing the offence, hence the appropriateness of a *nom de guerre*.

Pugin and Eastlake could not be said to be avant-garde. With the middle classes entrenched in their comfortable philistinism and their false principles, artists since, say, 1880 have operated on the fringes. With the concept of the avant-garde the idea of novelty became, at least for the time being, inseparable from progress in art. The idea that art has leaders and followers has imposed a structure on our imaginations which has been difficult to shift. Baudelaire presented a paradox which captures the contradiction inherent in the ceaseless quest for novelty: 'The chief task of genius is pre-

cisely to invent a stereotype.'

The avant-garde was a reflection of society's image of itself, but seen in a distorting mirror: decadent poets, wacky artistic types throwing paint in the public's face, slaves to the senses and brutes to their lover, were convenient inventions which in fact emasculated art by stringing a cordon sanitaire around artists, defining their territory as out of bounds. The dangerous Bohemian in hat and cloak with a fevered imagination behind a smouldering brow made glossy by absinthe and pale by late nights and later mornings had a trembling lower lip. Only the eyes were fixed with the singular purpose: *épater les bourgeois*! This was exactly what Albert Jarry did when he shocked the audience at the first performance of his play, *Ubu Roi*, with the opening line: 'Merde.' It is a measure of the durability of the avant-garde that nowadays this is almost all that is remembered of Jarry's script.

And later, when familiarity had dulled the shock value of the sleaze, the avant-garde found expression in another strange bird, but one of a rather different feather – the technocrat. Here again, in a rapidly industrializing world, there was an image both to lionize and to demonize. From just after the First World War avant-garde artists abandoned their fedoras, cheroots and dirty habits and became missionaries from another territory equally alien to the stay-at-home bourgeois: the laboratory and the factory. Whereas if you had been researching a television programme on the avant-garde in 1880 you would have had to go to Paris and sip wormwood liquor with oddball painters and poets while dancing girls demonstrated the contemporary deficiencies of laundering, by 1920 your producer would have had to send you to Germany to meet Hungarian *émigrés* in boiler suits teaching metal-work, photography and callisthenics to wide-eyed, flaxen-haired, firm-thighed delegates of the master race. Nowadays to discover the avant-garde, you have to look in history books.

In the nineteenth century art became a commodity, and the avant-garde was a reaction to this. Restless neophilia, supported by Baudelaire's romantic interpretation of the artist's purpose, is as much a product of consumer culture as kitsch, its mirror image. The two extremes help define the middle ground of consumer values. The feverish quest of the artist is to capture the beauty which Ezra Pound characterized as that evanescent gasp 'between one cliché and another'. The avant-garde rejects convention and taste is not so much disregarded as deliberately confronted. A certain sort of thin-lipped, joyless, overstuffed, polished taste existed in every Victorian parlour, even Freud's, and especially in those redolent with morality. The existence of the avant-garde had a curiously stabilizing effect on already conservative middle-class taste: if taste is a matter of choice and discrimination, what choice can there be when only the radically new is acceptable?

Henry Cole's century was as obsessed with the past as ours is with the new. Eclecticism in architectural style had put all of history into the market-place – to Mr Crumpet's distress. Henry Cole's false principles are one example of a search for meaning in a clutter of sense-lessly reproduced stylistic motifs. Adolf Loos (1870–1903), Viennese architect, polemicist and *fin-de-siècle* man-about-the-Ringstrasse,

Kitsch is not just a matter of taste; it can be defined. It occurs only in civilizations where choices are offered to the consumer.

'Culture is on the horns of this dilemma: if profound and noble it must remain rare, if common it must become mean.'

George Santayana, *The Life of Reason*, 1914

was one of those keen to reject the eclectic delusions of the nineteenth century which had so dismayed Crumpet. Loos wrote: 'Ever since humanity discerned the stature of classical antiquity, one single thought has united all the great architects. They think: I am building the way the ancient Romans would have done. We know that they are wrong. Time, place, purpose, climate and setting all make this impossible.'[20]

Loos saw the history of civilization in terms of mankind's progressive emancipation from ornament (a conceit more workable, perhaps, in Brixton than Vienna). He equated decoration with degeneration, pointing out criminals' liking for tattoos. It is not too fanciful to suggest a similarity between Loos's rejection of artifice and ornament and Freud's exposure of the devices and delusions which disguise the essential primitivism of the psyche. The extraordinary climate of Vienna about 1900 was, for a nation largely unaffected by the industrial revolution that brought us Mr Crumpet, the product of a crisis in classical reason.

This crisis, which we can see in what Freud thought, what Klimt and Schiele painted, what Schoenberg composed and what Loos built, produced extraordinary fertility in art and social science. It is perhaps worth cautioning that this splendid flowering coincided precisely with Austria's political and economic decline, and may, indeed, have contributed to it. No longer able, or even much inclined, to influence external events, artists became introspective and somewhat desperate. Freud excavated the soul, Klimt and Schiele made a sensuous and lascivious sort of eroticism into fashionable high art, and Loos tried to make architecture

systematic. Arthur Schnitzler, the most successful playwright of the day, whom Freud described as his *alter ego*, filled the theatres with his plays on sex, death and the soul. His best-known novel was called, characteristically, *Sterben* (*To Die*).

Meanwhile, adrift from any particular social group or class, avant-garde artists justified their elected alienation as a necessary tension-builder in the process of creation. As a consequence alienation became a test for high art, rather as drowning in witch trials was proof of purity. Simultaneously, a fashionable lack of content in abstract art (*c.* 1906–66), forced artists to develop exquisitely high standards of self-consciousness, self-reference and self-veneration. In painting, the generalized quest was for reduced form, a goal pursued at the expense of meaning and communication and in the teeth of public censure. Some painters, including Brice Marden, achieved total meaninglessness. Soon, public censure gave way to public apathy and indifference – and, for instance, to the founding of the Saatchi Collection, where avant-garde art was apotheosized in the service of social mountaineering.

Avant-garde is an extreme perversion of taste. Sometimes it is in dramatic confrontation with nostrums of good taste; at others, to take an absurd example in the work of a sculptor like Richard Serra, it is a triple distillation of refined good taste and therefore comes very near to being something else entirely. Under the despotism of the avant-garde, art was reduced to serial fads. In the age of postmodernism, which actually *depends* on copying and on restless neophilia, both the avant-garde and kitsch have become emasculated –

or become the same thing, depending on your point of view.

Although a diligent researcher would quickly find an early-nineteenth-century reference to the radical avant-garde,[21] the concept makes most sense when politics and art bifurcated, and that happened most convincingly in Vienna. The Viennese avant-garde, perhaps more so than any since, was both the product and the scourge of the bourgeois society that gave rise to it.

There have been many Whig interpretations of art history which draw facile connections between the artistic revolution of Vienna in 1900 and the social engineering which the modern movement attempted after 1920. The two are very different, but they share avant-garde characteristics in their pointed rejection of safe bourgeois taste. Heath-Robinson in *How to Live in a Flat* (1936) satirized the fashion for modernism:

Museums and galleries validate the tastes of their founders. Modern art died when it was kidnapped by New York's MOMA. In London, the Saatchi Collection (*below*) demonstrated the eternal validity of the truism that art follows money. The Saatchis were unusual in disdaining eighteenth-century French furniture and preferring minimalism.

Whereas formerly the best furniture was made by carpenters . . . the trade is almost entirely in the hands of plumbers, riveters, blow-pipers, and metal-workers of all sorts. As a result, the ultra-modern living room resembles a cross between an operating-theatre, a dipsomaniac's nightmare, and a new kind of knitting. The advantages of steel furniture, of course, are that it does not harbour worms, requires only an occasional touch of metal-polish, and can be bent into all manner of laughable designs . . . It is quite possible . . . to construct a chromium-steel dining-room suite in one continuous piece – that is, without lifting the pen from the paper. This can be moved bodily from room to room – and even set up on the roof, in the event of anybody wishing to dine there – in about one third of the time needed to shift an old-fashioned mahogany suite. Moreover, when the conversation at the dinner-table flags and all present are wondering what the dickens to say next, the host can create a diversion by inviting his guests to guess where the suite begins and ends, and awarding a small prize, such as a book of stamps or an unopened tin of peaches, to the winner.

A vegetarian lady novelist with a modernist rug.

The modern movement was an attempt to make the avant-garde *popular*, its leaders – unwittingly – imposing their own exclusive tastes upon reluctant populations. The vegetarian lady novelist sitting in a tubular steel chair reading Schnitzler in front of a rug with an abstract pattern was an easy target for conservative architect and moralist Sir Reginald Blomfield. In *Modernismus* (1934) he attacked the idea of novelty: 'What impresses us most in these struggles for something new, is not their originality, but their immodesty, the folly of thinking that it is worthwhile to abandon the beaten track and stand on one's head in the ditch in order to attract attention.' Blomfield deplored the fact that 'The Modernists blandly ask us to exterminate any aesthetic preferences and instincts we now possess, and offer ourselves as passive victims.'

Every page of Blomfield's coarsely argued text proves that he did not know of, say, Le Corbusier's romantic early work at La Chaux-de-Fonds (which the architect himself in fact suppressed). Those who did knew that Le Corbusier was engaged on a mission of continuous refinement, development and discovery. *Modernismus* is too simplistic a book to accommodate a more sophisticated analysis of the flawed ambitions of modernism, but Blomfield was right in questioning the exact standards by which the modernists declared their taste to be perfection: 'What we complain of in the propaganda of Modernism is its confusion of thought, its persistent habit of begging the question, and of laying down as accepted principles what are, in fact, merely dogmatic assertions.'

What the modern movement got wrong, in all its heroic special pleading, was its confusion of idealism with purpose, its mistaking paternalism for the commonwealth, and, as Baillie-Scott remarked, its impudent claim to having a monopoly of practical efficiency. If you were that vegetarian lady novelist in Cambridge *c.* 1930, you might well enjoy your tubular steel, your Schnitzler, and your non-representational rug, but that would be a matter of taste, not of scientific certainty. The assumption that the technical solutions to furniture and building design of 1929 were permanent was, as Blomfield said, based on mistaken sociology and arbitrary psychology. The icons of the modern movement were as historically specific as the nineteenth-century obsession with modesty, which led the Victorians to dress table legs in little pantaloons. Just as they felt it necessary to disguise household apparatus and buildings, so the modern movement demanded the clear articulation of an internal mechanism through external form.

But then Blomfield's objections to the modern movement were also a matter of taste – and his particular taste was influenced by snobbery: as a patrician grandee, he disliked the foreignness of modernism (hence the sly title of his book which he puts into the German form), and he disliked its Jewishness even more: 'I detest and despise cosmopolitanism.' Blomfield warned that the modernists' taste for order would not win friends and in its place he offered evolutionary traditionalism. Today it is axiomatic that the modern movement's absolute belief in the idea of progress was a weakness: sadly, new forms have not stimulated a revolution in the human spirit. Osbert Lancaster spoke for the majority when he wrote in *Here of All Places* (1958):

> This apparent failure of the reformers in the realm of domestic architecture is, one fancies, one of psychology. The open-plan, the mass-produced steel and plywood furniture, the uncompromising display of structural elements, are all in theory perfectly logical, but in the home logic has always been at a discount.

The modern movement was the most extraordinary international exercise of the avant-garde will. The fabled unwillingness of architects and designers to accommodate the tastes of the public was hardly calculated to ingratiate themselves with the toiling masses on whose behalf they made such extravagant claims. This version of the avant-garde failed, despite some powerful rhetoric and some magnificent monuments, to provide a widely acceptable unifying symbolic order. If the modernists had known Mr Crumpet better, they would have been aware that the explosion of mass-consumption meant the eternal loss of even the idea of a homogeneous society, and hence of a single value system.

The avant-garde only ever captivated the high culture of an intellectual élite (which has been aped by the social élite from Peggy Guggenheim to Doris Saatchi). But, as the art critic Clement Greenberg pointed out in an influential essay, *Kitsch and the Avant-Garde* (1939), 'Where there is an avant-garde, generally we also find a rearguard.'

Greenberg popularized the term, which until then had been almost exclusively the province of obscure German philosophers and aestheticians, such as Fritz Karpfen, whose book *Der Kitsch* (1925) was among the first on the subject. Kitsch – which comes from the German word meaning to cheapen – and the avant-garde look very different, but are correlative in substance: they are the equal and opposite manifestations of that unique historical awareness (Blomfield called it 'hysteria') which produced the concept of modernity. They are the fruits of bourgeois capitalist society in what Marxists call its decline and the rest are glad to

Left Mass-consumption meant no possibility of homogeneous taste. Modern architecture could never achieve the universality its creators demanded. Touchingly, it evokes not a socialist-utopian paradise, but élitist experiment.

Saddam Hussein's fascination with vulgar effect was such that he had a triumphal cast made, in Basingstoke, from models of his own forearms. He also commissioned the chief wizard of post-modernism, Robert Venturi, to design the Baghdad State Mosque.

see as its evolution. Just as the avant-garde places novelty and originality above all else, so banality and vulgarity are lionized in kitsch. Both violate everyday conceptions of good taste.

Kitsch is unthinkable without industrialization and feeds off it. Something kitsch almost invariably involves an adaptation from one medium to another, from appropriate to inappropriate, transformations made possible by advances in technology. It is all very well to have tongue-and-groove wood panelling, if that is what you fancy, because that is a matter of taste. Wallpaper looking like tongue-and-groove is, however, kitsch. Similarly, kitsch almost always diminishes size and scale. On sale in Japan, for instance, is a lavatory paper dispenser in the shape of Mount Fuji. Witless adaptation, diminution and relentless cheapening categorize kitsch.

In a funny way the achievement of nearly universal literacy in industrialized countries turned cultures that were once homogeneous into segregated classes. The virtuosi were a privileged élite with easy access to art, music and literature, and among this minority it was not difficult to settle on standards and expectations for art. By about 1900 reading and writing had become everyday skills. Literacy, according to Clement Greenberg, 'no longer served to distinguish an individual's cultural inclinations, since it was no longer the exclusive concomitant of refined tastes.'

Unable or unwilling to transfer peasant culture to the city, the new urban proletariat and petty bourgeoisie were equally ill-equipped to participate in the traditional high culture of one of Sir Joshua Reynolds's salons. Kitsch was, to use another German word of uncertain provenance but perpetual value, an ersatz version of high culture called into existence by a new form of demand. Greenberg, a left-wing champion of modernism, scathingly describes the trash sold to those he considers insensible to 'genuine' culture: 'Kitsch, using for raw materials the debased and academicized simulacra of genuine culture, welcomes and cultivates this insensibility. Kitsch is mechanical and operates by formulas. Kitsch is vicarious experience and faked sensations. Kitsch is the epitome of all that is spurious in the life of our times.'

Kitsch has the external characteristics of art, but is actually a falsification of it. The modernist view was that kitsch was unreflective enjoyment. At worst, kitsch was seen as a pernicious influence against which 'genuine' culture must be constantly vigilant. Not only is kitsch an inevitable consequence of industrialized society; it is dependent on mechanical and electrical reproduction for its existence and transmission. Kitsch is made in factories and consumed in bulk, growing the while; it blurs the distinction between art and life and supplies information in place of meaning. The hunting-scene formica place-mat is one example. A gilt chandelier is another.

There are different types of kitsch, but they all share an element of *inappropriateness*. A carpet woven in the pattern of an ornamented ceiling complete with beams and mouldings (shown at the Museum of Practical Art, London, 1852), an ashtray made of postage stamps (Museum of Art Indiscretions, Stuttgart, 1909), 1960s 'colonial' kitchen (Gillo Dorfles, *Kitsch*, 1969), Ronald Reagan's bedroom (1983) or the new Department of Health and Social Security Offices in Whitehall (1987) – what each example has in common is bad faith: each strives for an effect which is at odds with the true and proper purpose.

An instantly recognizable form of kitsch, as common today in Japanese restaurants serving sushi on wood-effect, plastic platters as it was a hundred years ago when a bar of chocolate was made to look like the Kaiser, is the transfer of a work of art to an inappropriate medium. Before post-modern architecture, this sort of nonsense was the definitive kitsch object, because it so manifestly undermined one of the highest forms of genuine culture – the original work of art. Mass reproduction of unique works is in itself a violation of one of the most precious tenets of Western art, and repro-

During 1987 toiling artisans painstakingly re-created bogus Victorian interiors for the ministers of the Department of Health. Here was kitsch furnished at taxpayers' expense to bolster the self-regard of pompous officials.

ductions applied to mundane merchandise heighten the violation of traditional values. The destruction of what aesthetes call 'the privileged moment' when a viewer communes with a unique work of art is caused by a debasing familiarity with reproductions. This applies to music as well as to painting (and to a lesser extent to architecture and literature – think of the mythical tourist who left a production of *Hamlet* because it was made up of old quotes).

The regular abuse of fragments of classical music in advertising sets up banal associations when the piece is played in full: for the time being at least, Bach's Air on a G String is inescapably associated with cheap cigars, the chorus from the last act of *Turandot* with an Italian airline. Recently, the post-modern architect Michael Graves has taken abuse of classical values further by endorsing cheap shoes in US press advertisements.

If the avant-garde is consciously individualistic and self-referential, then the expression of communal values is, by definition, anti-art, which is to say, kitsch. This is just one of the ways in which the avant-garde expresses its modernity when compared with the art of the past (whose highest aim was to articulate contemporary spiritual, philosophical or political ideals). It also explains why the political art of the twentieth century – one thinks of firm-thighed Nazi athletes, Soviet tractor drivers – is of necessity kitsch. Milan Kundera develops this idea in his novel *The Unbearable Lightness of Being* (trans. 1984): 'The feeling induced by Kitsch must be a kind the multitude can share. Kitsch may not, therefore, depend on an unusual situation; it must derive from the basic images people have engraved in their memories: the ungrateful daughter, the neglected father, children running on the grass, the motherland betrayed, first love.'

To the Victorians, as well as to the modernists, who in some curious ways resemble them, kitsch was irredeemable, but our less certain age is not so dogmatic. Kitsch can be rehabilitated by context, or at least by intention. In his book *Kitsch* (1969), Gillo Dorfles discusses the Manhattan skyline, which comprises many individual monstrosities, yet the overall effect is stupendous. But the extent to which a sophisticated environment can transform the meaning of the objects it contains prompts Dorfles to caution, 'This is why we will never be altogether sure that fake marble columns, papier-mâché statues, wood imitation wallpapers, glass animals from Murano and even mother-of-pearl shells and Brazilian hardstone in the shape of ashtrays, although themselves undoubtedly Kitsch, are beyond recovery.'

The deliberate cultivation of outrageous bad taste has long been a favourite device of the avant-garde. A sly, knowing sophistication at odds with safe bourgeois values suggests that an excess of good taste is just as lamentable as evidence of bad. Taste which is too good is a tell-tale of conformity and insecurity, what George Bernard Shaw called moral cowardice. In this exquisitely balanced equation the amount of admissible bad taste is subject to fine measurement by social scrutineers. Artistic, aristocratic and wealthy élites set their own rules, but ordinary citizens have to be more cautious. There is a parallel in the well-rehearsed cycles of fashion: a suitable amount of time must have passed for a revival to be acceptable, but there is a fine line between being at the forefront of a revival and simply being out of date.

As soon as it loses its original offensive impact, avant-garde hyper-kitsch is soon subsumed into the mainstream as another 'school' for art historians to ponder and catalogue. In the early 1980s the most radical Milanese designers, including Alessandro Mendini and Ettore Sottsass, were producing furniture for Studio Alchymia and for Memphis, whose designs were calculated to offend. Andrea Branzi used patterns derived from Mondrian and Kandinsky paintings on his *poltrona falsa* because they were 'good and cheap'; Mendini spoke boastfully of his *galleria del copismo*. By

the time these gaudy, banal bastardizations of
1950s suburbanism artfully contrived to
oppose every assumption of the modern movement had been included in more than 200
international glossy magazines and had
appeared in Karl Lagerfeld's Paris apartment,
they had become just another style of rich
man's chic. Now used everywhere, from Victoria bus station to department stores and food
packaging, the Milanese movement, which
started as an ironic gesture by Sottsass, soon
became, quite appropriately, the most celebrated cliché of recent years.

Memphis was a reminder that contemporary
eclecticism differs from nineteenth-century historicism in this regard: today everything
quickly becomes a cliché and therefore potentially kitsch. Like post-modern architecture, of

In ironic day-glo, self-conscious kitsch becomes cool.
Memphis refuted positivist progress and – for a very
brief, witty moment – achieved celebrity. The effect
was the final rejection of modernism, whose stern
forms were then subsumed into a gallery of copies.

which it is a poor relation, Memphis refuted positivist faith in progress, and, defined negatively in opposition to modernism, signalled only an ironic awareness of the end of all movements. Its media success was fuelled by the notion that popular culture is at odds with the high or genuine stuff. Before the assumptions of modernism were regularly called into question, the self-appointed guardians of the avant-garde derided popular taste. Thus Virginia Woolf snobbishly stigmatizes the hapless middle classes: 'The true battle lies not between the highbrows and the lowbrows joined together in blood brotherhood but against the bloodless and pernicious pest who comes between . . . Highbrows and lowbrows must band together to exterminate a pest which is the bane of all thinking and living.'

Highbrows believe that they alone can appreciate culture. Good taste in their interpretation is constantly under insidious attack from the philistine lowbrows with their coarse pretensions (which continuously threaten the exclusivity of highbrow culture). Clement Greenberg was a highbrow. Until very recently highbrows could write without irony this sort of condescending gobbledygook in the pages of *The Partisan Review*: 'Middlebrow culture attacks distinctions as such and insinuates itself everywhere . . . Insidiousness is of its essence, and in recent years its avenues of penetration have become infinitely more difficult to detect and block.'[22]

Meanwhile, the highbrows (defined by A. P. Herbert as the sort of people who look at a sausage and think of Picasso) are happy to patronize the lowbrows, listening to their jazz and taking an interest in their 'vernacular' art

High culture
Interest in creative process and symbolism
Preference for experimentation
Introspection preferred to action
Accepts different levels of meaning
Expects consideration of philosophical, psychological and social issues

Upper middle culture
A less literary verbal culture
Figurative and narrative art preferred, especially if illustrative of individual achievement or upward mobility
Enjoys nineteenth-century art and opera, but not early music or contemporary art

Lower middle culture
Form must unambiguously express meaning
Demands conclusions
Unresolvable conflicts not made explicit
Interested in performers, not writers or directors
Influenced by word-of-mouth judgement

Low culture
No concern with abstract ideas: form must be entirely subservient to content
Demands crude morality with dramatic demarcations, but usually limited to family or individual problems
Performer is paramount; enjoys vicarious contact with 'stars'
Considers ornateness attractive

Adapted from Herbert J. Gans, *Popular Culture and High Culture*, 1974

'I don't like the words "good taste". I almost prefer the words "bad taste". Good taste is dictated by the Diana Vreelands in life. You have to wear this, you have to wear that. You're short and fat, but you have to wear Calvin Klein clothes that don't suit you. This business of taste is something to question. I think people should develop their own taste through education, by really working on it. They should study and go to museums, not just for something to do, like going to the movies, but really to understand our heritage. They should make certain that whatever they have is truly meaningful to them, that it isn't just some bric-à-brac. Most homes are full of meaningless things. Most houses you go to you will not remember as you would remember another type of interior – a restaurant in Paris, for instance. They're just splendid and not necessarily done by a decorator.'

Ward Bennett to Barbaralee Diamonstein, *Interior Design*, 1982

or their cooking. The lowbrows do not threaten because they are uninterested in highbrow values.

What is most interesting in this discussion of the self-evident is the precise mechanism by which the dominant classes impose their own distinctions between high and low, or 'good' and 'bad'. To Baudelaire, bad taste was 'intoxicating' because it offered the aristocratic pleasure of not pleasing, thus confirming that whenever taste is discussed, notions of class cannot be too far away. Snobbery is one of the most effective mechanisms by which this dominance is maintained. The manifestations of snobbery, or turning class into performance art, are also often taken to be 'good' taste. Listen to Harold Nicolson in *Some People* (1927): 'Sir Sidney Poole had asked me to dinner: Mrs Lintot had called me by my Christian name: and the Grand Duke Boris had said, quite distinctly, '*Monsieur, j'ai connu votre père* . . . Lady Dury had bought a Tang horse.'

Had Lady Dury just bought a Thermos flask, Nicolson would not have thought it worth mentioning. Snobbery is a remarkable and profound invention, an institution at least as formidable as the prison system and certainly as characteristic as the age that created it. It can be attributed to Thackeray and dated quite precisely to the years when the laws of consumer culture were being established; *The Book of Snobs* was published in 1848. Snob was undergraduate slang for low-bred and – in a device later adopted by Nancy Mitford – Thackeray made it plain that it is snobbish to worry about snobbery.

Critics transferred this social game to the world of material things, where it became known as 'good' taste. Deadly competition burst out about what objects mean. It is remarkable how very charmless things regarded highly in 1850 appear today. Here is further proof that taste changes. When Owen Jones dreamt about interior design in *The Grammar of Ornament* (1856), 'There are no carpets worked with flowers whereon the feet would fear to tread, no furniture the hand would fear to grasp, no superfluous and useless ornament which a caprice has added and which an accident might remove,' his ideas sound astonishingly prescient, but the quickest glance at what Owen Jones himself designed shows that the words themselves flatter modern ears only to deceive contemporary eyes – his designs look as hideous as much of the stuff he reviled. While he praised those things in which 'nothing could be removed and leave the design equally good or better', the passage of time demonstrates that a good deal remained to be removed from designs of his own making.

The terms good taste and bad taste do not represent absolutes, but their usage is distinctive and telling, since it reveals the preferences and prejudices of particular social groups. They are crude ways of assigning value to things, but their validity derives only from the power and prestige of the social group that uses them. Most often, the value is not inherent in the object itself, but in the intention of its consumer. If good taste means anything, it is pleasing your peers; bad taste is offending them. But cultivated bad taste, or kitsch, can achieve either result.

Taste is more to do with manners than *appearances*. Taste is both myth and reality; it is not a style.

Part Two

SCENARIO

ARCHITECTURE

Painting the Lily

'Taste, taste, taste,' the architect Frank Lloyd Wright once remarked; '*cows* have taste!' His idea is clear: in the proper practice of architecture taste plays no part. Successful building arises out of something other than socially or culturally conditioned aesthetic preference, most probably from fundamental principles of design and laws of construction. Andrea Palladio could mend a smoking chimney *and* design a façade with the orders artistically orchestrated into major and subsidiary divisions, creating a beautiful, functional whole the while.

Ever since refinements in engineering separated the practical from the artistic in building and made anything that was imaginable possible, architectural design has been virtually reduced to a matter of taste. Given recent advances in construction technology, buildings will stand up with or without architects. Fast-track building has, quite literally, left design behind. Modern buildings, with their computer floors and voids, their vast provision for data-cabling, are not stand-alone monuments like the Duomo in Florence, or Grand Central Station in New York, but merely evanescent architectonic hardware with a finite life. In big new corporate developments, where the building itself is not intended as an *advertisement* – the big corporation puts its marker down on Fifth Avenue or in the Square Mile – it is, with its spaghetti of fibrox cables and its line of sight microwave dishes, merely an adjunct to the company's telecommunications budget.

In fast-track building construction begins before the design process is complete, so that, in inflationary times, the expensive bits get under way first. First there is the piling, then

Most contemporary commercial architecture is pure kitsch, inspired by the vulgar intention of impressing with flashy materials and costly effects. Meanwhile, the architecture goes on behind.

the structural steel, then metal floor decks, then pouring concrete for floor slabs. When the frame is complete, windows, curtain walls and insulation are fitted at the same time as the mechanical and electrical services. If there's a moment left over, someone designs a snazzy shape so the clients think they've got some 'architecture' for their money.

In the United States it is accepted practice for a developer to hand over only the decorated shell, core and public spaces to the tenant, who then has to hire an 'interior architect' to finish the job. While Brunelleschi laboured to make the details and the proportions of the Pazzi Chapel in Florence evocative of something like divine peace, the First Republic Bank of Chattanooga, or Get Rich Quick plc, needs a structure with a life of fifteen years, which can be appreciated at 55 mph from the freeway or while stationary in the congealed traffic of the City of London. If at all possible, the insides betray the thrusting ambition of the chairman of the board. With such an ugly disjunction between form and technique it is scarcely surprising that the greater part of contemporary architecture is pure kitsch.

At a time when, despite appearances, aesthetic considerations are secondary to the imperatives of finance and technology, there have been few more eloquent demonstrations of a crisis in taste than the rise of the royal household to outspokesmen on the arts and architecture. This, in Britain's case, alas, is a few centuries too late. Although the Prince of Wales's discovery that architecture is more than mere building and his consequential intervention into the public debate were welcomed, the fact that the House of Windsor has never commissioned a new building of substance or value illustrates the very symptoms of the malaise the Prince of Wales wished to cure. Not since Prince Albert – of whom Arnold Bennett observed, 'He has a lot of taste . . . all of it bad' – has a member of the royal family been so concerned with art, architecture and design. Although his views are occasionally contradictory, by virtue of his special prestige the Prince of Wales has set out on an extraordinary adventure: to become an arbiter of taste.

Incensed by the apparently thoughtless brutality of much 'modern' architecture, Prince Charles has called for a 'revival' of classical architecture. In a curiously contemporary version of the pathetic fallacy, the prince suggests that aping the architecture of Hawksmoor will take us, balance-of-payments deficit and all, back to the graceful world of the salons, with the plinkety-plonkety elegance of a Scarlatti sonata to accompany our reveries. It is a pleasing idea, but a misleading one.

But the prince's taste for classical architecture is a modern one and has no sanction from the past; as Viollet-le-duc said of restoration, '*Le mot et la chose sont modernes.*' *What* exactly is the royal understanding of classical architecture? Whatever they may now think of it in Kensington Palace and Highgrove, classicism is not a style that has always enjoyed universal approval. In *The Stones of Venice* (1851–3) John Ruskin excoriated the genre:

> Let us cast out utterly whatever is connected with the Greek, Roman or Renaissance . . . It is base, unnatural, unfruitful, unenjoyable, and impious. Pagan in its origin, proud and unholy in its revival, paralysed in its

> 'So why not capitalize on many people's desire for an environment of character and charm, which is also more conducive to reproductive work because the surroundings make you feel better? This is very much the age of the computer and the word-processor, but why on earth do we have to be surrounded by buildings that look like machines?'
>
> Prince of Wales, speech at the Mansion House, London, 1987

old age . . . an architecture invented . . . to make plagiarists of architects, slaves of its workmen and sybarites of its inhabitants; an architecture in which intellect is idle, invention impossible, but in which all luxury is gratified, and all insolence is fortified.

Inigo Jones's Palladianism was great architecture in that it achieved a unity of structure and style and could have admitted no alternative. The revolution in building technology made fundamental changes in the assumptions of architecture: four centuries after Jones, Cesar Pelli's Canary Wharf was architecture reduced to cladding.

Prince Charles's call for a revival of this colourful phenomenon came at a moment of transition, not to say uncertainty, in British life. The royal polemic, aimed chiefly at plan-

ners and developers, assumes that there are certain aesthetic absolutes (the Prince calls them guidelines) which the powers that be, or at least were, have ignored in their pursuit of profit. Of the planners: 'As things stand, they are only justified in rejecting a proposal if it is absolutely hideous; anything merely ugly must be allowed to get through.'[1]

What the Prince of Wales said was remarkable not only for its outspokenness, but also for the questions it begged (some listeners claim to have detected more than a hundred). Signifi-

cantly, no mention was made of the question of taste. The prince's aesthetic guidelines were presented as universally attractive – a high-handed (if not high-minded) version of the popular theory that, but for the cravenness of the public and the wickedness of the planners and developers, the cityscape of London in the late twentieth century would be as attractive as people imagine it to have been three hundred years before (when the streets were sewers of horse shit and corpses). It was not the first time that revolutionaries and royal families shared a desire to turn the clock back.

It does not take long to deconstruct the Prince's message. The subtext presents an imaginary city built when aesthetic principles were better understood by palace and pauper alike. He argued for a limitation on the height of buildings, a proscription of certain materials, advocated the proportion of windows, and even the requirement to build in a certain style; such rules gave us Georgian London and would allow St Paul's to dominate the skyline of the capital. All very well, provided you *like* Georgian London and accept the dominance of Christian classical architecture in our cities as sempiternal.

Of one particular development, Paternoster Square, close to St Paul's, Prince Charles said:

Let there be an informative exhibition showing the area as it *was* [my italics], the plans of Wren, Hawksmoor and Lutyens ... It should be a beautiful area on a human scale, built at ground level not on top of a car park. I'd like to see sheltered arcades, courtyards, a public square, with small shops and businesses at ground level – above all to

London's Paternoster Square was a heroic, if flawed, essay in sixties' planning, not shown to advantage by its proximity to the universally admired St Paul's Cathedral. It became a celebrated cause when, after the intervention of the Prince of Wales, its redevelopers abandoned the stern principles of architectural design and adopted narrative themes apparently inspired by Walt Disney *mouli*ed into craven pastiche.

cater for the needs of, and to create something special for, the three million tourists
who already visit St Paul's each year . . . I
would like to see the medieval street plan of
pre-war Paternoster reconstructed, not out
of mere nostalgia, but to give meaning to
surviving fragments like Amen Court and
the Chapter House, now left like dispos-
sessed refugees in an arid desert of godfor-
saken buildings. I would like to see a roof-
scape that gives the impression that St Paul's
is floating above it like a great ship on the
sea. I would also like to see the kind of
materials Wren might have used – soft red
brick and stone dressings perhaps, and
the ornament and detail of classical
architecture.

Prince Charles may have a clarity of vision
and purpose; this muddle-headed argument for
a tourist trap of quaint, cute architecture must
be attributed to a confusion of advisers and is
perhaps best undermined by reference to one
assertion alone. How appealing and charming
'soft red brick' sounds, how humane and desirable. Yet structurally efficient brick is not significantly softer than concrete, and Victorian
board schools and workhouses tell a different
tale about the seductive qualities of brick. The
Prince of Wales may have become a remarkable popular champion; he may, like Cocteau,
have lied to tell the truth; but his criticisms of
architecture reveal as much of the tastes of his
caste as they do of his insights into modern
technology.

The concern to recapture 'character and
charm' is peculiarly located in a specific time
capsule: London, according to the Prince of

Wales, was fine in the seventeenth and eighteenth centuries. Contemporary Manhattan, it
is suggested by omission, not so. Paris during
unspecified periods, fine. No mention of Germany or Italy (save one eighteenth-century reference to London being at least as noble a city
as Canaletto's native Venice). Buildings lower
than the entablature of St Paul's are fine;
ancient monuments should necessarily be preserved; technological culture is bad.

To some this may be a backward-looking,
sentimental farrago of special pleading, but in
it lies the germ of the idea that the observance
of rules will produce better architecture. Architecture has almost always been subject to rules,
but in the past they have arisen not from ideal-
istic princes looking for a responsible role, but
from the influence of a religion whose values
were universally accepted; the dominance of a
ruling caste whose authority was complete and
total; the overwhelming force of technological
innovation; or from a combination of all three.

The rules of the Greek architects at the
height of classical civilization were technical
and mathematical, part of a tradition that can
be traced back to the period of Homeric myth.
They adopted a repertoire of form and detail to
masonry instead of timber. In the early Middle
Ages Carolingian architects developed the stern
engineering principles of Roman buildings,
creating memorable symbolism in the *West-
werk* of their churches, which led to the great
Gothic cathedrals. Their architects used every
available innovation in technology to express
in their buildings a universal aspiration
towards God. And, as Rudolf Wittkower has
shown in his *Architectual Principles in the Age
of Humanism* (1947), Renaissance architects

depended on cosmology and geometry for the formal and spatial perfection of their buildings.

Palladio refined the rules of all preceding versions of classicism into what for many people are the most pleasing buildings ever made. In the eighteenth century – a godless age – architects were particularly interested in achieving aesthetic perfection through the study of proportion. Georgian taste derived from the Renaissance and from the early seventeenth century, when house-trained classicism, imported from Italy, began to attain a generalized respect. The 'Georgian' period in English history produced buildings so universally admired because client, architect and builder tended to share a point of view; they were intent on making the most of *contemporary*

possibilities, and were fortunate to find a language of design that was honest to the available building techniques and expressed their intentions. To copy the soft red brick and the classical details is to mistake effect for cause.

The modern movement of the twentieth century can be seen, at least from the perspective afforded by an approaching millennium, as an attempt to re-establish classical rules forgotten during the wild party of Victorian architectural excess. As Sir John Summerson put it, the modernists 'had an authentic sense of reaction. They had seen that the environment was detestable and that they could change it.'[2]

Prince Charles and Le Corbusier have this in common: they both believe that better architecture depends on rules. Neither is available for interview, but each would probably deny that his preferred rules are merely culturally and socially conditioned preferences. In fact, each has eloquently expressed his own version of taste in architecture.

The rules of taste have been blown apart by the twentieth-century revolution in building techniques. The contemporary debate in architecture hints at a complex underworld of ideas that support the English perception of self and culture. In the rhythms and textures of English life you can detect the idea that elsewhere there is a dream world that can somehow become accessible. A short cut to it involves putting classical doo-dads on otherwise unremarkable buildings.

The landscape of this dream world is picturesque: nature is benign and the only man-made interruptions are comely country houses. Of all the great things the English have invented,

Left   The Georgian period in architecture produced buildings universally admired and continuously aped, except by technicians fastidious about sanitation and thermal efficiency. Every *parvenu* requires a Georgian house.

Below   The idea of the country house consumes the British imagination, thereby retarding thoughts of progress.

according to Henry James, the well-appointed, well-filled country house is pre-eminent. Perhaps he would have said the same about motorway queues of well-appointed Range Rovers loaded with kit for the country weekend.

Besides leaving us with an unforgettable sense of loss, the First World War nurtured the irony which underpins and undermines so much of English culture. A generation brought up on certain expectations of landscape, on certain attitudes to nature, and to abroad, found poppies and heard lark song in the foul mud of Flanders. As self-defence in the trenches they read Greek poets and eighteenth-century writers: pastoral literature provided escapism from the most hellish of circumstances. When the survivors returned, their sharp appetite for the eighteenth century was gratified by country houses, sometimes inherited, sometimes newly built. It is not fully appreciated that the cult of the 'Georgian' country house is in fact an architectural invention – some would say whimsy – of the twentieth century.

All prospects of social or material progress in England are bedevilled by this taste for historical retreat. Hence the Range Rovers (whose first advertising literature made a very self-conscious appeal to the hunting and fishing set). Most Englishmen of a certain class would prefer to live in a shoddily built, thermally inefficient, insecure travesty of classical architecture than commission a new house in a city.

Modern architecture was frustrated in England because the country had a vast stock of fine, authentic old buildings, and those who don't already possess them seem determined to acquire or replicate them. To the existing

Neo-Georgian offices in Wapping. One architectural style above all others appears to suggest probity, dignity, reserve and other characteristics so inappropriate to modern business. An example of high aspirations and hack tastes.

inertia provided by an inventory of architectural treasures has been added the dead-weight of backward-looking convention: new old houses are also being built. The fact that the English largely disdain any form of innovation in architecture is sure evidence of an imaginary national Arcadia which, the true believers maintain, might be imperilled if rational building were ever to be taken seriously.

Quinlan Terry is the most articulate spokesman of the new country-house movement, the architect in the van of the long march back into history. His eloquence is explainable, since he claims direct inspiration from God, but – just to be sure of his credentials – has established for himself a fake Palladian style, as inappropriate in twentieth-century building as a periwig and the locutions of Alexander Pope would be in broadcast journalism. None the less, the ham quality of Terry's designs pleases his philistine clients, who cannot see that his architecture fails to match the efforts of the humblest jobbing Georgian builder. It is perhaps just as well that Terry says, without apparent embarrassment, 'I do not design for the masses.' Terry's every remark betrays the assumption that architecture is the province of the monied, land-owning classes (as sex was once said to be): in a recent debate he demonized 'borrowed money' in his assault on modern architecture.

There is a whole literature to validate, quantify, record and give credibility to the English obsession with country houses. One decade after the First World War, Christopher Hussey, country houses editor of *Country Life*, published his elegant book *The Picturesque* (1927), a learned study of an earlier episode in the

Quinlan Terry's Richmond Riverside is low-brow architecture for those who have middle-brow talent but think they are high-minded. Failing to match in any respect the talent of the crudest jobbing Georgian builder, Quinlan Terry debases the currency of architecture. His work is very popular.

history of taste which the English could not forget. A parallel development was the skilful hijacking of the National Trust by James Lees-Milne and others: a body created by Fabian socialists to preserve the landscape of England was converted by rhetoric and social prejudice into a club determined to preserve the architectural memorials of a certain age and a certain class. This magnificent act of preservation retarded English architecture for the good of no one save those people already living in country houses and weekend tourists in Volvos who buy jam and kitsch tea towels with printed illustrations of Blenheim and Chatsworth.

The privations of the Second World War also produced an intense nostalgia for the mythic country house, described so flavoursomely in Evelyn Waugh's *Brideshead Revisited* (1945). But in his Preface to the second edition of 1960 Waugh registered his dismay at the way in which the country house idea had become exploited and debased:

> It was impossible to foresee . . . the present cult of the English country house. It seemed that the ancestral seats which were our chief national artistic achievement were doomed to decay and spoliation like the monasteries in the sixteenth century. So I piled it on rather, with passionate sincerity. Brideshead today would be open to trippers, its treasures rearranged by expert hands and the fabric better maintained than it was by Lord Marchmain.

Waugh is saying that the country house idea has become phoney: if we consider an old country house that has been restored, then what we are looking at is a sly and artful

The privations of the Second World War inspired an intense longing for the country house. The National Trust was transformed from a utopian-socialist environmental movement into a popular club for Brideshead revisiting.

confection; if new, it is a pretentious one. Yet the magazine *Country Life* has grown and grown and in so doing has created a market for fantasy architecture publications, only partly satisfied by the recent appearance of *Country Homes and Living* and the short-lived *Landscape* (revealingly, despite it title, almost entirely about country houses). Their constituency has grown too, and now extends far beyond the original hedging and ditching territory; these magazines are popular guides to a culture that is more *arriviste* than its zealous champions would want you to believe.

Not only is the 'Georgian' country house a recent innovation in the history of architecture (Victorians preferred massive, gutsy, castellated piles, stinking of the strength, wealth and power of the brewery and soap fortunes that so often built them), but its interior design, while appealing persuasively to a sense of the past, bears little relationship to true historical precedents.

There will be more of this in the next chapter, but it is worth relating here that John Fowler, who joined Lady Colefax to form Colefax and Fowler in 1938, the firm of interior decorators which is the *locus classicus* of the style, was not an architect, landowner or scholar, but a furniture salesman from Peter Jones department store in Chelsea. The basic assumption of interior decoration, as someone remarked of the trade's doyenne, Elsie de Wolfe, is to introduce new money to old furniture. It is England's loss that the relationship does not work the other way.

Since the end of the Second World War there has been plenty of old and new money spent on country houses. The roll-call of leaders of

Right above Counterfeit architecture. Robin Leigh-Pemberton, Governor of the Bank of England, assiduously built himself a reproduction house. It is quaint that old money had to fake such a coinage.

Right below In Britain revulsion for the future is so universal that even government ministers are accommodated in bogus Tudorbethan style.

English life capable of seeing quality in building only when it evokes a past that never existed is as impressive as it is depressing. Robin Leigh-Pemberton, now Governor of the Bank of England, built himself a breathtakingly accurate and bogus William and Mary house at Torry Hill, near Maidstone, just before 1960. While he would discourage the forging of banknotes, Leigh-Pemberton felt it proper for a man in his position to live in a sly reproduction.

Two decades later, Michael Heseltine, then Minister of Defence, hired Quinlan Terry to build a garden pavilion in Northamptonshire. The style was amateur-dramatic-society Palladian pastiche – the architectural equivalent of the minister having troops descend from Westland assault helicopters carrying halberds and flintlocks. When one landowner, the Duke of Westminster, actually built himself a modern country house at Eaton Hall near Chester, he was excoriated by another (the Duke of Bedford). In a telling line, he said that such a style might be appropriate for a bypass in suburbia, but it certainly was not for a gentleman's seat. The Westminsters are now creating a new 'old' country house at Eaton. In the context of this debate it is clear that 'appropriate' is rich shorthand for the symbols and aspirations of a certain class and their imitators.

When at the end of 1987 the largest government buildings since the Second World War were revealed in Whitehall, the Minister of Health's offices were not in the new works (styled to look 'modern', like the Abu Dhabi Hilton) but in the painstakingly restored and reconstructed Richmond House wing. At the end of the twentieth century ministers of the Departments of Health and Social Security will be occupying expensive, fake Victorian rooms furnished to bolster their assumptions and self-regard by tax-payers.

Revulsion against the modern world was given another form with the creation of suburbia. The English had to invent suburbia because after the First World War there were too many people who couldn't face modern life in the city, but who couldn't afford a time capsule in the country. Since 1964 prime ministers have been suburban socialists or suburban meritocrats and it is significant that John Fowler designed the interiors at Chequers, in Buckinghamshire, the official country house of the prime minister. His pretentious style suited their parvenu taste – what the French call *petit goût* (to distinguish it from the opposite and equally laudable *bon goût* and *mauvais goût*).

One theory of cultural history suggests that ideas originating near the top of the social-political-intellectual pyramid trickle down to the bottom and influence the populace. This model is perhaps too simplistic (as society, politics and the intelligentsia tend to be completely distinct pyramids), but in any case it has been upended. At a time when the Prince of Wales and his advisers aim to arbitrate about taste, his mother, the Queen, has given to her second son Andrew, Duke of York, a perfect small monument to suburban *petit goût*.

There is nowhere more suburban in England than Bracknell, in Berkshire. It is the home of those multinational lares and penates, 3M, Honeywell, Avis and British Aerospace. A few miles beyond the ring road in the walled garden

The stagnant taste of suburbia has achieved minor miracles of domestic smugness . . . at the expense of architecture.

of Sunninghill Park, on land owned by the Crown Estate Commissioners, the Duke and Duchess of York have had a new house built. As the first new royal house since Balmoral and Sandringham it is a noteworthy event, but at this transitional moment in the development of English architecture, Sunninghill is especially interesting. Consciously so or not, it is a manifesto of contemporary aesthetic and social values.

The architects have chosen a style that is not Georgian, but, if anything at all, Texas Tudorbethan, reminiscent of certain suburban prototypes, familiar in Ilford and Wembley and Fort Worth. Gables and ridges dominate the skyline and some decorative timberwork compounds what the Duke of Bedford would have

'What happens to the really awful presents, or the spare salt cellars and ink wells that flood into Buckingham Palace? HMS *Britannia* is the final resting place for bizarre gifts. The Queen admitted in her sixtieth-birthday broadcast to hanging a whale's tooth in the day cabin. "Too kind," the Queen would have murmured, as she accepted the memento on a Commonwealth tour. And that is what she would have said to Sheikh Rashid of Dubai, when he produced a solid gold camel beside a palm tree hung with ruby dates. It is on the dining table of the *Britannia*.'

Suzy Menkes, 'Present and Correct', *Majesty*, August 1986

called the bypass effect. From a long, low building chimneys rise picturesquely above the line of the ridge. From the south a smaller gabled pavilion gives on to a patio and conservatory. The fixed point in this joke oak architectural blur is the Duke of York's helipad. Like government ministers, he does not disdain those twentieth-century innovations he finds most convenient.

The regression at Sunninghill from the eighteenth century to an earlier, albeit imprecise, age is significant. It tells us as much about contemporary taste as did the Duchess of York's wedding list, which, according to the *Daily Mail*, included 'nothing modern or freaky'. Harold Brooks-Baker, editor of Burke's Peerage, writing in that newspaper, said of their choice of fake Georgian furniture, hunting-scene place-mats and pheasant ornaments in silver with gold inlay, 'This is the wedding list of an eighteenth-century Prince

Above   The hunting-scene place-mat: definitive kitsch both for suburban dining-rooms and City boardrooms.

Left   The British Royal Family has built little this century. The Duchess of York's new house outside Bracknell may have been inspired by the television series *Dallas*.

who never intends to get up and an old-fashioned bride who never expects to cook.'

The royal family's architectural taste helps to sustain an image of an England not so much gone for ever as having never existed – until now. 'Comfortable, timeworn, eccentric and elegant . . . That's English country style . . . the beauty, romance, nostalgia and originality of these houses . . . have evolved over many years. From their lovely examples . . . you will be inspired to bring the distinctive look of the English country home into your own.' The words are those of an advertisement for a new picture book, perhaps noticed by the Duchess of York, which appeared in a Sunday edition of the *New York Times* in 1987.

The suggestion is that we are not concerned with technology, function, rules and principles, nor with the search for democratic excellence so movingly and persuasively described by Walter Gropius in his own *apologia*, *The Scope of Total Architecture* (1956). Rather we are to engage in a nugatory quest for a mythic Arcadia and in a round of competitive social display where you score triple points for philistinism.

It is usually forgotten – or perhaps not realized – that beauty often arises out of the proper husbandry of the design principles our culture eschews. The artificial and easy creation of cosy, styled time capsules, whether by Colefax and Fowler, Quinlan Terry or the Duchess of York and her advisers, is as futile an occupation as the search for a new colour, or the purblind quest for historical recovery. M. H. Baillie-Scott, the arts and crafts architect who contributed a catalogue of forms and details to the repertory of suburban building, wrote in *Houses and Gardens* in 1906:

> To consciously aim at achieving 'style' in design, either old or new, is to follow a Will o' the Wisp. For the pursuit of style, like the pursuit of happiness, must necessarily lead to disappointment and failure. Both alike are essentially bye-products, and the quality of the bye-products is in direct ratio to the worthiness of the ideal pursued. One may liken style to the jewel in the hilt of a sword, which flashes brightly when the blade is drawn in a worthy cause and to which the warrior absorbed with the matter in hand will give but slight attention . . . he

who aims at style is he who would paint the lily rather than watering it.

Yet country house enthusiasts – inspired, according to one, by 'artistic appreciation and nostalgia, combined with social curiosity and a strong dose of snobbery' – will speak of the charm of the elevation and the comfort of reading about a house like your own in a glossy book advertised in a New York newspaper.

This is not perhaps sufficient reason, justification or excuse for derivative details, unexciting forms, complacent and unimaginatiave plans and a witless reliance on safe, familiar materials and details. Every pronouncement about country houses and classical revivals – whether from conservationists, the Prince of Wales, or, via Quinlan Terry, from God himself – speaks volumes about taste. The English care not about the art and science of building, but about offering up a certain set of social values and principles; country houses and the version of life they sustain say more about Britain than modern architecture ever can.

Dishonesty entered the world of architecture in the nineteenth century when, for the first time, the whole of history became available to ambitious *nouveaux riches* whose capacity to get anything done far outstripped their powers of judgement. In every case they chose a historicist style in order to give credentials to their very recent achievements.

Perhaps the outstanding example of this was the castle style. Nineteenth-century authors were well aware that Walter Scott was trying to gain a 'pedigree' by having Edward Blore build a pseudo-baronial castle for him at Abbotsford, Roxburghshire, in 1816. The

Nineteenth-century beer barons, press lords, soap peers and even literary knights assumed a castle style for the domestic quarters. Walter Scott's Abbotsford was a ridiculous perversion of architectural history.

architect, C. R. Cockerell, while an admirer of Scott's novels, wrote that 'I cannot help attaching an idea of ridicule to these mock castles which can never fulfil the notions one has of the times in which they were built.'

Yet you could fill a book with examples of gentlemen's houses in the castle style . . . and of literary allusions to them, from John Bunyan's 'Doubting Castle' to Robert Browning's 'castle, precipice encircled/In a gash in the wind-grieved Appenines'. But as the Church of England hymn is perhaps the most powerful literary form created by the Victorians, Cecil Francis Alexander provides a telling example. In 'All Things Bright and Beautiful' (1848), which offers sure evidence of current typology, the significance of the lines 'The rich man in his castle/The poor man at his gate' is painfully clear.

Bodelwyddan in Wales is typical of the bogus castle style. An Elizabethan house, it was classicized about 1800, according to the taste of the times, and then castellated about 1830. Samuel Beazley, an obscure architect, could claim three castles in the same decade: between 1833 and 1838 he built Leys Castle, Inverness; Studley Castle, Warwickshire; and Caher Castle in Ireland.

The taste was not, of course, restricted to England, although in France and Germany the reasons for building or rebuilding *châteaux disparus* or *verfallene Schlösser* were usually more directly romantic: Gustave Doré's illustrations to the 1873 edition of Balzac's *Contes Drolatiques* give the example in one case, while the Schloss Lichtenstein, just off the Karlsruhe–Mannheim autobahn, inspired by Wilhelm Hauff's 1839 novel of the same name, gives

the other. What could better suggest the inheritance of history, of blood-lines going back to Charlemagne, than a house dressed in fake medieval military architecture?

In his biography, *The Whims of Fortune* (1985), Guy de Rothschild describes the building of his family seat at Ferrières, just outside Paris, which was transformed from a modest country seat to an architectural manifesto of the *nouveau riche* sensibility. *Nouveaux riches* had been scorned since Molière, but in the France of the *Directoire* and the Empire a new class of speculators and adventurers came into being. With money to spend, they overshadowed the traditionally penurious aristocrats, yet wished to be seen in exactly the same light. James de Rothschild, Guy de Rothschild's great-grandfather, 'decided to build a residence on this domain worthy of his success and social ambitions – no doubt also a subconscious symbol of revenge by a former ghetto child'. An *émigré* in France, he built in pseudo-

English style. (And when Ferdinand de Rothschild, an *émigré* in England, bought Waddesdon Manor, near Aylesbury, from the Duke of Marlborough in 1874, he built a pseudo-French Renaissance château. Exotic validation has ever since been a *nouveau riche* technique of acquiring a form of status that cannot properly be tested.)

Whether Guy de Rothschild was aware that his analysis of his grandfather's motivations anticipated Charles Revson's coldly impressive remark, 'Living well is the best revenge', is not clear from the context, but it is a significant contribution to the anthology of remarks which further an understanding of the *nouveaux riches*; William H. Vanderbilt's 1883 remark to a reporter – 'The public be damned'

'Le goût Rothschild' – once described as 'plutophilia' – illustrates the absurdities of *arriviste* taste. In France the Rothschilds built a vaguely English country house at Ferrières (*left*); in England they built an absurdly ugly French-style château at Waddesdon (*below*).

– is also typical of the genre.

Ferrières and its thousand acres of grounds was designed by Joseph Paxton and completed in 1859. The house has its own place in architectural history and the gardens theirs in the history of landscape. In a discussion of taste, it is the interior contents and arrangements that are most revealing of how wealth distorts the meaning of things. In 1893 the *Pall Mall Magazine* observed: 'The houses of the great, the decoration of their tables, their dinners, their dresses, their carriages, all are followed by every class, with a fidelity only limited by their pecuniary ability.' Much the same thing, although less well and thoroughly done, might today be found in Beverly Hills, Rose Bay, Wilmslow or Virginia Water.

The interior at Ferrières was decorated by a minor painter, Eugène Lami, in a manner we might call Napoleon III mish-mash: a heroic assemblage of earlier styles and motifs. The 'white drawing room' was in the style of Louis XVI; tapestries were hung against a white background, white marble statues framed the windows and *trompe-l'œil* angels floated on the cloud-scudded ceiling. In the next room, the *salon des cuirs*, a Govaert Flinck hanging of *The Triumph of David* was translated on to individual Cordoba leather panels, creating what Guy de Rothschild described as a seventeenth-century effect, modified somewhat by Italianate Renaissance marble columns. The main drawing room had a huge wooden Bavarian fireplace. Pure kitsch.

The main hall, top lit by a device of Paxton's, housed most of the pictures. James de Rothschild's attitude to art may be understood from the fact that he commissioned Ingres to paint five copies of his wife's portrait, a vulgarizing gesture cut short by the revolution of 1848. There were also van Dycks, Gainsboroughs, works by Frans Hals, Roman portrait busts, armour, a billiard table, Italian cabinets inlaid with ebony, ivory, marble, onyx and semi-precious stones, a piano, an eclectic assortment of furniture, and tables groaning under the weight of artfully arranged precious objects. Quite without irony Guy de Rothschild says the effect was one of 'harmonious disorder':

> Perhaps this is what the decorators and antique dealers describe as the 'Rothschild' style, alluding to an atmosphere that is found in most of the homes inhabited by members of my family: a Napoleon III décor, personalised not only by all sorts of *objets d'art*, but above all by a sense of comfort and intimacy which intermingles furs, flowers, plants, family photographs, precious miniatures and rare books.[3]

Just as the Rothschild's establishment at Mentmore had modern amenities including hot water, central heating and artificial forced ventilation, the guest rooms at Ferrières were exceptionally well appointed, with private bathrooms and canopied beds. Each room was upholstered with 'pheasant', 'bird' or 'bouquet' fabrics. When the King of Prussia came to stay he remarked, 'What an incredible place! A king would not have dared to build it. It took a Rothschild!'[4]

Upstaging royalty and getting praised for it has been the aim of all *nouveau riche* taste ever since. When Napoleon III himself visited Ferrières in 1862 (dressed incongruously in the national costume of Brittany), Baron Roths-

child arranged for the chorus of the Paris
Opera, with Rossini conducting, to perform
'The Death of the Pheasant' at a shooting
dinner.

Parallel with the creation of new country
houses for the new rich, made prosperous out
of banking, beer or patent medicines, was the
development in cities of new ways of living –
in apartment blocks and in hotels not intended
for the rich but for the merely prosperous: their
architectural styles and their internal arrangements speak volumes about contemporary
taste, about the expectations we have from
architecture and from building services.

The most impressive hotels of the early nineteenth century were American. Charles
Dickens described Boston's Tremont as only a
'trifle smaller than Bedford Square'. Bourgeois
expectations were expressed not only in terms
of style and architectural arrangements, but
also in terms of manners: at the Grand Hotel
in Northumberland Avenue of 1881, the management unusually allowed – even encouraged
– non-residents to eat at the *table d'hôte*. London's Grosvenor Hotel of 1860 was built,
'appropriately' for the continental rail ter-
minus, in a French Second Empire style, with
pavilions designed to impress at the ends of the
massive roof structure.

In New York, Edward S. Clark, head of the
Singer Sewing Machine Company, built the
'Dakota' apartment block on Central Park
West before the park was finished. A sort of
proto-urban country house it was so named
because of its remoteness. Soon, however, the
Upper West Side was full of apartment blocks
which, in the terminology of the time, were
known as hotels. The Hotel Lucerne of 1904

In New York and London the urban hotels of the
nineteenth century introduced a new, itinerant class
of 'consumers' to the experiences of architecture,
interior design and modern services. Then as now,
leading hotels were either museums or laboratories
of taste.

on West 79th Street is typical. The Hotel
Charlesgate of 1891 on Beacon Street in
Boston benefited from the introduction of lifts.

The hotels and apartment hotels anticipated
some of the developments codified by that
extraordinary phenomenon known as the
modern movement in architecture and design.
Like the fashion for country houses, the
modern movement was inspired by the First
World War; its history has been exhaustively
choreographed by an international troupe
including Nikolaus Pevsner, Bruno Zevi and
Kenneth Frampton. In the context of taste in
architecture modernism is significant as a
return to rules, an attempt to redefine classical
order, after nearly a century of fumbling
experimentation.

The Shock of the Ordinary

Simplicity was a novel addition to the choices
available to a new consuming urban public. In
Austria, a country relatively primitive in industrial terms, since the 1850s Michael Thonet
had been mass-producing bentwood furniture
which matched technique to purpose to achieve
a timeless harmony which seemed to elude
other manufacturers, and which provided a
model for architects and theorists, including Le
Corbusier. It was in Austria too that Adolf
Loos adapted arts and crafts views about
simple materials, blended them with his own
slick and idiosyncratic version of the manners
and fashions of the English gentleman, and
turned them into a philosophy which was to
be profoundly influential on the taste of the
modern movement.

When Loos wrote in *Ins Leere Gesprochen*

The Thonet No. 14, used and admired by Brahms,
Lenin and Le Corbusier, among many others.

(1898), 'Which is worth more, a kilogram of stone or a kilogram of gold?' he was addressing himself not to the *nouveaux riches*, who had their own answer, but to architects, who, he believed, should view all materials as equally valuable. This conceit anticipated by a decade Loos's best-known remark, usually misquoted, in which his taste for simplicity reached its exquisite extreme: 'Not only is ornament produced by criminals, but also a crime is committed through the fact that ornament inflicts serious injury on people's health, on the national budget and hence on cultural evolution.'[5]

The taste for simplicity in design (and, indeed, in life itself) led architects throughout Europe and America to see the machine both as a means of achieving the longed-for rational modern design, and as a metaphor for that achievement. This romantic attitude to the machine is itself an expression of taste, not the unalterably correct approach to design which its proponents believed it to be. The first half of the twentieth century is alive with mechanistic imagery: to Stalin artists were engineers of the soul; to William Carlos Williams a poem was a machine made of words. The machines which inspired architects then were the elemental ones employing beautifully clear and uncomplicated Pythagorean geometry and Newtonian mechanics; the modernist philosophy could not sustain the change from applied maths to non-linear equations which came with electronics.

Like Functionalism (with which machine romanticism is sometimes confused) it is a point of view that is being expressed, art aesthetic preference that is being proclaimed, rather than a univerally valid set of laws being revealed. Berthold Lubetkin wrote in *Building*

Adolf Loos, architect and pamphleteer, who wrote 'ornament is crime'. His cultivated minimalism was the exact complement to the Vienna of Schiele, Klimt and Werfel.

Design, 'Such a mistake to call it Functionalism . . . it is the wrong word, people think it means a mechanistic approach when there is so much more to architecture – love and beauty.' The romance of the machine is a distinctively twentieth-century phenomenon – in the nineteenth century buildings (and machines) were often disguised. At the turn of the century in Germany the Deutscher Werkbund began promoting the concept of *Typisierung* – a process of standardization – and in response to it the architect Bruno Paul designed *Typenmöbel* (furniture which sounds far more aesthetically advanced than it looked). However, the most rigorous innovations came about during the First World War, or as a direct result of it. In 1916 the Deutscher Normen Ausschuss (later developing into DIN-type approval) came into being. Perhaps the most remarkable, if least obvious, innovation of the DNA was the introduction around 1921 of A-standard sizes for stationery used by the Reichskuratorium für Wirtschaftlichkeit in its efforts to impose standardized book-keeping for all German industries. The architectural equivalent, in terms of function and utility, was the social architecture of Erich Mendelssohn and Ernst May, and the polemics of Bruno Taut. Reminiscing at the end of 1987, Sir John Summerson, who was influential in bringing modernism to Britain, said that Bruno Taut's book *Der Sieg des Neuen Baustelles* was 'what crystallized modern architecture for the first time into a unified movement for me.'

Crystallized or not, a great deal of serious nonsense was spoken about functionalist architecture, although it did produce some heroic buildings. The first European housing estates,

Right above   Philip Johnson, a wealthy socialite, became the leading US architect in post-war years. Like Betjeman in England, he opportunistically supported modernism as long as it was élitist. His own summer house was a *tour de force* of inspired plagiarism, built in the chic community of New Canaan. Johnson later repudiated the style that made him famous.

Right below   California has often attracted European *refusés*. Rudolph Schindler unsuccessfully attempted communal living, long an unrealized totem of the modernist experiment.

Terence Harold Robsjohn-Gibbings was an American decorator who cheerfully satirized foibles of architectural taste.

the *Siedlungen* of Bruno Taut himself, for instance, were, according to Philip Johnson and Henry-Russell Hitchcock, too often built 'for some proletarian superman of the future' (*The International Style*, 1931). Between 1921 and 1922 Rudolf M. Schindler, a Viennese *émigré* in the United States, built himself a house on Kings Road in West Hollywood that was the sort of building which T. H. Robsjohn-Gibbings later satirized in his sly book *Homes of the Brave* (1954). Schindler, tired of a weary and corrupted Europe, saw southern California as a new frontier where a perfect life would be possible. Here he built a Utopian dwelling, a collection of independent studios opening on to private gardens. The architectural design was intended to radicalize all conventions: two families shared the one dwelling and did a time-share in the kitchen. Schindler designed striking but ergonomically hostile furniture. There were no conventional bedrooms, but 'sleeping baskets' on the roof. These baskets were in fact simple frames, covered with canvas in the event of rain. The Schindler house was quite mad.

The symbolism of efficiency reached its extreme in the middle period architecture of Le Corbusier. (That he was on a campaign is indicated by his pseudonym: Le Corbusier is the *nom de guerre* of Charles-Edouard Jean-neret.) Heavily influenced by his contact with Germany (where he had worked in Peter Behrens's studio), Le Corbusier was responsible for the century's most romantic and poetical expression of contact with the machine. The austere German *Typisierung* was translated into the more chic *objet-type* – the Thonet No. 14 chair, the standard wine goblet which Le

Corbusier used in his paintings and in his interiors. 'Mass production demands a search for standards. Standards lead to perfection,' he wrote in *Vers une architecture* (1923). He believed that engineers were 'healthy and virile, active and useful, balanced and happy in their work' and he coined the ultimate expression of the taste for things mechanical in calling houses machines for living in, just as the aeroplanes he so admired were machines for flying in. (Frank Lloyd Wright's riposte was 'Yeah, just like a human heart is a suction pump.')

Despite misquotations, despite being plagiarized by talentless hacks, Le Corbusier's influence was so powerful that the story of architecture for most of the twentieth century has been

Le Corbusier's Pavillon de l'Esprit Nouveau at the Paris exhibition of 1925. With its international style architecture, Thonet furniture and purist paintings, here was an exquisite moment in European civilization.

the story of whether you accept or reject his view of the world, which is to say his taste. No single building truly by the hand of Le Corbusier exists in either England or the United States (although New York's United Nations building has some claim), but for sixty years his was the dominating vision – until a recent change of taste has tested his assumptions and found them wanting by some contemporary standards.

Vers une architecture appeared in England in 1927 as *Towards a New Architecture*, published by John Rodker, whose distinguished avant-garde list included the first editions of T. S. Eliot's 'Ara Vos Prec', Ezra Pound's

Lutyens was the English Le Corbusier. Both men were architects of original genius, but while Le Corbusier worshipped technical reason, Lutyens enjoyed traditional wit. Each synthesized a long tradition in their native cultures.

'Hugh Selwyn Mauberley', the first translation of Lautreamont's *Chants de Maldoror*, and a proposal for James Joyce's *Ulysses*.[6] The translator of *Towards a New Architecture* was Frederick Etchells, a Francophile aesthete who made ends meet during the translation by doing make-weight designs of fake Georgian houses for the Grosvenor Estate. In his introduction to the English edition Etchells wrote:

> A man of today, reading this book, may have the impression of something akin to a nightmare. Many of our most cherished ideas in regard to the 'Englishman's castle' – the lichened tiled roof, the gabled house and patina – are treated as toys to be discarded, and we are offered instead human warrens of 60 storeys, the concrete house hard and clean, fittings as coldly efficient as those of a ship's cabin or of a motor car, and the standardised products of mass-production throughout.

It was a brave statement from someone who was to publish a somewhat different book, *The Architectural Setting of Anglican Worship*, in 1948, but a number of disclaimers (and some subtle cuts) were sufficient to encourage even the doyen of English country-house architects, Sir Edwin Lutyens, to review the book favourably. Lutyens could see that Le Corbusier was not an austere Trotskyist intent on eradicating the past: both the cadences of his prose as well as its content recall Viollet-le-duc, the greatest of French architectural thinkers. Similarly, while Le Corbusier has been demonized in recent years as an inhumane brutalist, no close reading of his writings nor a close examination of his buildings could support this analysis.

'Simplicity is not equivalent to poverty; it is a choice, a discrimination, a crystallization. Its object is purity. Simplicity synthesizes.'

Le Corbusier, *Précisions sur un état présent de l'architecture et de l'urbanisme*, 1930

If during his heroic period – from, say, 1917, when he settled in Paris, to the mid-1930s – purification of architecture was his ambition, the resulting purity was sensuous and beautiful, not arid. In *Précisions sur un état présent de l'architecture et de l'urbanisme* (1930) he declared: 'Simplicity is not equivalent to poverty; it is a choice, a discrimination, a crystallization.'

According to Le Corbusier, modern decorative art is not in fact decorated, and, like Sir Henry Cole or Gustav Pazaurek, he made his choices clear: Thonet, filing cabinets, aeroplanes – good; Lalique, Galle, Sue et Mare – bad. But Le Corbusier did believe, at least for a while, that the laws of architecture which he was revealing would eradicate questions of taste. There was, he might have said, no alternative. Although his career changed and developed continuously, Le Corbusier's reputation has been a victim of his own rhetoric.

The post-modern revisionists require him to be seen as an austere 'functionalist' intent on reducing life to hydrocarbons and Bolshevism, yet even his villas of the 1920s, when his designs were at their most austere, were inspired by a symbolic vision similar to that which inspired Wren and later Prince Charles. The difference is that the source of Le Corbusier's vision was the modern world (which is why he illustrated cut-away drawings of racing car stub-axles in his artistic journal *L'Esprit Nouveau*). His buildings actually looked like the Farman biplanes and ocean liners he so admired.

The mistake has been to treat Le Corbusier as if he were a monolith, but this can at least be interpreted as respect for his overwhelming stature. His various and articulate detractors have preferred to regard him as such because a monolith is simpler to tackle, if not to destroy, than rambling settlements. Vision is more easily neglected. The extent of Le Corbusier's ambition and the dimensions of his artistic achievement can best be judged by the significance attached to the demonstrable failure of his vision in recent years, even though he was not actually responsible for those international urban blights: town planning, urban motorways, skyscrapers, overscaled city centres, regimented apartment blocks and built monotony. Alas, as Ada Louise Huxtable remarked, 'Eventually, the acceptance of modern architecture came about through a combination of technology and economics that was able to achieve what lessons in taste and morality could not.'[7] Towards the end of his life Le Corbusier himself remarked, 'Life is right and the architect is wrong.'

Le Corbusier was convinced that form was a manifestation of tangible concepts and laws. From this it was but a short step to conclude that perfection was attainable, which would eliminate the embarrassment of choice for ever. But late in life he began to understand that what he once believed was unalterably good, perfect and true – the law of machines – was in fact no more than a particular, even if very persuasive, aesthetic preference. Postmodernism has done more for journalism and publishing than it has for the history of architecture, but it has at least made frank discussion of wilful (and frequently illiterate) aesthetic preferences commonplace.

The prelude to post-modernism was the celebrated failure of modernism. In Britain, if a little less so in the United States, Le Corbusier and modern are virtually synonymous. St Louis's infamous Pruitt–Igoe development, dynamited by despairing city officials in the 1970s, is a realization of Le Corbusier's 1930 Radiant City proposal. And how very hostile and dull it seemed when transferred from paper to an urban lot. Similarly, in Britain, the municipal concrete brutalism of post-war urban 'renewal' actually became the official architecture of the welfare state. It was a reaction against this which produced buildings dressed up to be what they are not, occupied by tenants pretending to be what they are not, designed by architects using a vocabulary they did not understand.

Transvestite architecture

Given the background, it is perhaps not surprising that post-modernism owes most not to a great architect or patron, but to Charles Jencks, an ambitious American journalist living in London. Jencks established the scripture of post-modernism in his various hyped and hyping books: *Meaning in Architecture* (1969), *Modern Movements in Architecture* (1973) and *The Language of Post-Modernism* (1977). Another architectural journalist, Gavin Stamp, perhaps thinking of these very books, called post-modernism 'grotesquely vulgar, illiterate'.

Its chief monument is the AT&T building in New York, which dates from the last years of the giant corporation before courts executing anti-trust legislation broke up the old monopoly. A memorandum from Louis O'Leary, assistant vice-president of public relations at AT&T, to the architects, Philip Johnson and

Unlike a mild occasional preference for wearing inappropriate clothes, post-modernism becomes a perversion when it replaces all other drives.

John Burgee, is so extraordinarily revealing of taste in late twentieth-century architecture that it bears reproduction in full. Here is O'Leary describing the corporation's vision of itself, as expressed in the building:

> If we had our portrait painted, it should be by Norman Rockwell.
> If we were ancient builders we would have built the Roman aqueducts instead of the cathedral of Notre Dame.
> If we were a baseball team, we would be the New York Yankees, not the L.A. Dodgers.
> If we drove race cars, we would be Richard Petty, not A. J. Foyt.
> If we were a state, we would be midwestern, probably Iowa. Twenty years ago we would have been Nebraska.
> If we were a US general, we would be Omar Bradley, not George Patton.
> If we were a tree, we would be a huge and utilitarian Douglas Fir – not a Sequoia, and certainly not a Dogwood.
> If we could choose an epitaph (never believing such a thing would be needed) we would choose 'Millions of customers, but it served them well and one at a time.'

A building designed along these lines would have been a colourful affair, but Philip Johnson ignored the implied directive and instead preferred to satisfy Chairman John deButts's playful, innocent whim to own 'the world's greatest skyscraper'. It is a measure of deButts's sensitivity and humility that the skyscraper headquarters, unveiled on 30 March 1978, was part of a publicity programme initiated after an

Left The AT & T building in New York, intended to be the 'world's greatest skyscraper for the world's greatest corporation'.

opinion poll in 1972 had revealed to his dismay that less than 2 per cent of the US population recognized his name. So much for architecture being frozen music. Architecture has become frozen public relations.

Johnson was already New York's most celebrated corporate architect. He had secured the support of a younger generation as keen to ape his social position as he had been to imitate Mies van der Rohe's architecture. They included Robert A. M. Stern, Frank Gehry, Michael Graves and Robert Venturi. By exercising his considerable gift for patronage, without necessarily being patronizing, Johnson recommended each camp follower for important commissions.

William Shirer hinted at the darker side of Johnson's political motivation in *Berlin Diary*. Rich, clever, vain, patrician, and proud to be largely without principles or scruples – 'Remember, son, I'm a whore,' he once told me, and a lot of other people besides – Johnson had briefly practised a polished form of modernism of the Bauhaus sort. His office on the thirty-seventh floor of the Seagram building, which he designed with Mies van der Rohe, was until recently full of Barcelona chairs and Frank Stella paintings, but it is probably true to say, as Johnson himself once did, that he liked Mies's architecture because it was easy to copy. He gave further evidence of the philosophy that informs his life and work in a BBC interview of 1965: 'What good does it do to believe in good things? It's feudal and futile.'

Johnson's departure from the Bauhaus aesthetic was emphasized by the evacuation of his office from the Seagram building into his own 'Lipstick' building at 53rd and 3rd, which he

Amor vacui. Mies van der Rohe, architect of Park Avenue's seminal Seagram building, said, 'I don't want to be interesting, I want to be good' – the aesthetic of St Thomas Aquinas applied to the lobby of a drinks company headquarters.

Post-modernist competitiveness turned buildings into symbols, and the skyline became the focus in the image stakes. Hugh Stubbins's Citicorp building was one of the least compromised and most successful.

described as an oval building in a square environment, an architectural one-liner whose tiresomeness demonstrates the dominant superficiality of post-modernism.

In creating his monumental pastiche for AT&T Johnson achieved the remarkable double of satisfying both the largest and most conservative American corporation ('The last thing in the world we want is to be trendy,' declared Edward M. Block, AT&T vice-president) and the tiny, self-styled claque of radical post-modernists who, like Robert Venturi, were pleased to describe the profession that had once occupied Ictinos, Callicrates, Michelangelo, Bernini, Wren and Soufflot as 'decorating sheds'. Once the positivist ethic and aesthetic of modernism had been reduced to no more than a temporary aberration, everything was available for copying.

Johnson's experience in Berlin may have stimulated his taste for the monumentalism of Albert Speer, Hitler's architect. His AT&T design is for a 36-storey building 650 ft high (less monumentally, you could expect to get sixty floors into that height). The cladding consists of 13,000 tons of granite to cover up the fast-track steel-work – and to look just like masonry. Even the lifts were going to be granite inside. Inspired by the 1922 Chicago Tribune Tower competition (where Adolf Loos, of all people, submitted an entry in the form of a giant Doric column), Johnson wanted to advertise his break with modernism by abandoning the canonical flat roof and putting something else in its place. Nearby, Hugh Stubbins had done this brilliantly with his massive, single pitched condensor roof for Citicorp, immediately raising the stakes for corporate statements in Manhattan skylines. For AT&T Johnson chose a broken pediment, somewhat like a Chippendale chair. (Later, in 1984, with similar kitsch vulgarity, he built the Pittsburgh Plate Glass tower with a profile like Barry's Houses of Parliament.) That everybody in the vicinity of Citicorp had to reject a flat roof, even if they couldn't think of anything smarter, was demonstrated in 1987, with the completion of Helmut Jahn's Park Avenue Tower whose daft open-work pyramid has to light up at night in order to achieve an effect.

'We were classicizing,' Johnson said in a subsequent interview, one of many about AT&T. Thus he called the orifice in the broken pediment an orbiculum. He pretentiously compared the AT&T lobby with Alberti's church in Mantua, and made his admirers gasp at his range of educated historical reference. More sensitive people cringed at what Ada Louise Huxtable called 'a monumental demonstration of quixotic aesthetic intelligence rather than art'.

The ultimate test of a building is the quality and validity of the idea that sustained it. Postmodernists talk of Alberti, but what they are really concerned with is public relations, gratifying philistine clients and winning cheap aesthetic thrills. In an article in the *New York Times* Paul Byard, vice-president for architecture at New York's Architectural League, explained that,

Except for some institutional work, virtually the entire province of new design has been left to corporations indulging their wealth in headquarters monuments of little perceivable social utility or to developers chasing wealth by meeting demands for products at the outer margins of the market. The result is profoundly debilitating for a profession that is ethical at its core.

Post-modernism is not about ethics, it is about effect. Robert A. M. Stern in his *New Directions in American Architecture* (1969) argued for historical allusion, context and ornament. Fair enough, but they demand educations that are not patchy, sensibilities that are as wide as they are deep, and qualities of imagination and inventiveness that are all too rare. Mies van der Rohe might have been easy to imitate, but Lutyens, who knew how to innovate with traditional elements, whatever sins are committed in his name, also said, 'You can't copy.'

The generation of architects who survive the garish, opportunistic blotchiness of post-modernism are faced with the challenge of moving on, as Le Corbusier did, from the modernism of the 1930s, without denying its achievements, without taking refuge in a house in the country and without creating more transvestite architecture.

There are few architects able or willing to produce buildings that are absolute and true, few prepared to commit themselves to the realization of contemporary possibilities. Few find new clothes for new ideas. Construction technology has devalued art; clients buy big-name architects rather than designs; never before have taste and technique been so distinct. Never has the public been so interested in architecture; never has it been so disenchanted with architects.

INTERIORS

Vacuums of Taste

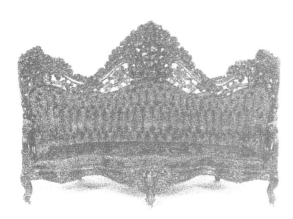

Viewed holistically, interior design is a travesty of the architectural process and a frightening condemnation of the credulity, helplessness and gullibility of the most formidable consumers – the rich. Yet it is a fascinating phenomenon in the history of taste since a study of it reveals in the most explicit way much of the normally hidden structure of our value system.

Like all other episodes in consumerism which put style in front of substance, interior design had its origins in the United States where it was and still is practised with the greatest professionalism, flair and consequent vulgarity. Americans enjoy interior design for the same reasons they enjoy Coca-Cola: because, lost in a vast continent free of any but the most recent traditions, they crave symbols and symbolism.

A distinguished English peer told me that twenty years ago when he was invited to parties in New York the hostess would introduce him to an East Coast politician; ten years later he would be shown off to a fashionable academic, but nowadays what he hears is, 'You *must* meet Norbert [*gnaw-bear*] Poubelle [*pooh-bell*]. *He* makes curtains!'

The story epitomizes the rising status of the interior designer. Now that only department stores and Japanese insurance companies can afford to buy paintings, and since there are few opportunities to build palaces, the interiors of private houses are empty canvases where fantasies can be created and lived out. But interior design is required only in houses where the owners have no eye or capacity for discriminatory judgement of their own. Writing in *Industrial Arts* in 1936, Duncan Grant condemned the nascent profession: 'The wealthy flat owner, distrusting his own taste, engages the "experts" of a furniture shop to design, deliver and dispose about his rooms the elements which, as the expression of his own individuality, would have made it a home.'

There have long been firms of upholsterers and decorators who could create entire interiors. 'I have never met with a class of men who were so hopelessly confirmed in artistic error,' Charles Eastlake wrote in his *Hints on Household Taste* (1868).

The interior designers' brief goes beyond providing furniture; they provide an image of self (both their own and their clients'). This is their age.

Linley Sambourne House in Kensington. In this cluttered glory-hole, belonging to the illustrator of *Punch*, the influential Victorian Society was founded.

Edmond de Goncourt, writing in the late nineteenth century, after half a century of disruption in values relating to interior design, noted,

> I have often said that if I were not a man of letters, if I had not got money, my chosen profession would have been to invent interiors for rich people. I should have loved being allowed to have my own way by some banker who would have given me *carte blanche* to work out the décor and furniture of a palace with just four bare walls.

The decline in influence of the Grand Tour and the explosion of mass-consumption contributed to the deregulation of classical order and produced High Victorian styles which, now gloomy, now glorious, were a symbol of the end of Taste with a capital T.

The requirement to have somebody else choose your domestic environment, either by default or by commission, originated in what J. E. Panton called the 'evil days' of the nineteenth century, when the new middle classes in England and the United States made terrible mistakes on a budget. In her book *From Kitchen to Garret – Hints for Young Householders* (1890), Panton describes how mass consumption brought new and debased aesthetic standards. The graceful eighteenth-century furniture of Sheraton and Chippendale was discarded, put in the attic or sold at a country auction to end up in a pub or the back room of a shop. 'And the heavy "handsome" furniture of mahogany and damask bore down upon us, and made us for a time the most depressed people, heavy with our ugly furnishings, and the mock of all nations that had

better taste and lighter hearts than we were possessed of.'

Panton's rhetoric is dolorously moral, befitting the conspiracy of 'good form' and propriety which after the death of Prince Albert in 1861 became codified into what we now call Victorian values. The age when parlours were stuffed with cherry-red Genoa velvet on cloth of gold, burnished brass, carved wood, gratings, swags of excess and a petrified forest of ormolu and damask was the age of the decoration of deceit. Soon electric light would reveal the clutter and dusty drabness of the surroundings, and *horror vacui* would become *amor vacui*. The fact that the people who lived in these dens of brown nastiness were the very same who needed and bought etiquette books confirms the link between taste and morals in consumer society.

The Habits of Good Society (undated but *c.* 1850) advised 'gentlemen' not to spend more than a tenth of their income on their wardrobe, which should consist of: seven pairs of trousers, seven coats, four morning waistcoats and one evening one, as well as gloves, linen, hats, scarves, ties and boots. And all were dark. Like Venice in 1460, London around 1860 developed strict, if unspoken, sumptuary laws (whose ghosts are with us today). And the same deadly conformity applied to the middle-class interior.

Besides electric light, one other technical innovation prepared the ground for radicalizing interior design: the mass-production of furniture, and in this area the name of Michael Thonet is outstanding. Johannes Brahms used one of Michael Thonet's new bentwood chairs while composing at the piano. Lenin used them too, as did Le Corbusier. Lately, they have been used in smart New York restaurants, but not for the same reason.

Michael Thonet (1796–1871) was born at Boppard, near Koblenz in Germany. He trained as a cabinet-maker and experimented with the technique of lamination – glueing together thin strips of wood (or other material) proved stronger than using a single piece of wood. Lamination was also cheaper and more effective than hand-cutting for making curved structures. Thonet's first essays in laminated furniture were admired by Prince Metternich on a visit to Koblenz in 1841, and he suggested that the market was more propitious in Vienna. Thonet settled there, receiving an imperial monopoly in 1842 and supplying the popular Café Daum in 1849.

Rising wages in Vienna forced Thonet to find a means of reducing the cost of making furniture using the labour-intensive lamination technique. His radical departure was to bend solid wood with steam. The parts of the chair were turned before they were steam-bent, and this innovation led to real mass-production furniture. A factory was established at Koritschan in Moravia to manufacture his No. 14 chair – the Vierzehner – in enormous quantities: a hundred million had been made by the time the Thonet company switched to tubular steel in the mid-1920s.

The construction technique demanded simplification: the Vierzehner was made of six separate pieces of beech. The cross-section of each component varies continuously at any given point according to the demands of the structure. At the 1862 London exhibition, where William Morris was displaying his pseudo-

Thonet's furniture, like Palladio's architecture, transcended taste because its form and content were in perfect harmony and balance.

A *bergère* armchair by William Morris, whose fantastic re-creation of pseudo-medieval art, literature and social theory set back British economic development.

medieval, pseudo-vernacular furniture, the jury, getting a sense that the evil days might be over, declared of Thonet's design, 'An excellent application of a happy thought ... they are not works of show, but practical furniture for daily use – they are simple, graceful, light and strong.'

While the technique certainly influenced the design, the style of Thonet's Vierzehner (as well as its less popular catalogue mates) is in fact a product of the taste for the rococo that influenced Viennese craftsmen around 1840. In Thonet's case clever and efficient development of technology subordinated this influence to the larger purpose of his furniture, whereas a similar influence acted as a deadening burden on his remarkable contemporary, Johan Heinrich Belter.

Belter (1804–63) was born in Hanover and trained as a cabinet-maker. In 1833 he emigrated to New York where he set up in business in 1844. He may have been as ingenious as Thonet, but American taste compromised him. James Fennimore Cooper had written to Horatio Greenough that in America, 'You are in a country in which every man swaggers and talks; brains or no brains; taste or no taste. They are all ex-nato connoisseurs, politicians, religionists, and every man's equal and every man's better.'[8]

In such an environment, Belter could not simplify, he had to complicate. In 1847 he took out a patent for 'Machinery for Sawing Arabesque Chairs' and another in 1858 for the 'Improvement in the Method of Manufacturing Furniture'. This second patent related to the industrial application of lamination, but Belter did not make the technique explicit; he dis-

guised it with grotesque and exaggerated carvings, sometimes politely known as rococo
revival, but more nearly comparable to the
louche decorations popular in New Orleans
bordellos. The determination to suggest
antiquity, even in so debased a form, calls to
mind Henry James's remark about Hawthorne:
'It is only in a country where newness and
change and brevity of tenure are the common
substance of life, that the fact of one's ancestors having lived for a hundred and seventy
years in a single spot would become an element
of one's morality.'[9]

Belter's furniture and his 'parlour sets' were
so popular that his name became a generic for
any elaborately carved and upholstered furniture, however it was made. It dominated local
taste until a remarkable woman called Elsie
de Wolfe (1865–1950) had a better idea. Like

Bordello style adapted for middle-class American
taste. In Europe, mass-produced furniture was decent
and spare, like Thonet's. Its technical equivalent in
America was the absurdly ugly furniture of J. H.
Belter, whose decoration is as much an offence to the
mind and the eye as to the bottom.

Owen Jones, she believed that there were principles of taste, but while Jones perhaps overestimated the public's appetite for inspiration from history and nature, Mrs de Wolfe's great achievement was to establish her aesthetic preferences as a saleable popular commodity, at least among a certain trashy, privileged class.

All the Looeys

While it would be a mistake to pursue the observation until it hardened into a theory, it is nevertheless irresistible to declare that, given historical perspective, interior design appears to be an almost exclusively homosexual activity (at least, from the supply side). In this respect, as in so many others, Elsie de Wolfe created the stereotype of the profession.

In a very curious way – and one which both parties would have repudiated – Mrs de Wolfe, an actress, predicted the tastes of the modern movement. The sensibility she confronted was created at least partially by the American influence of Charles Eastlake's *Hints on Household Taste*. His popularity led to a style known laconically as 'Eastlake walnut'. In his splendid Preface to the US edition of *Hints*, Charles Perkins – one of Boston's own tastemakers – wrote: 'Nowhere is modern sterility in the invention of form so marked as in America . . . We borrowed at second hand and do not pretend to have a national taste. We take our architectural forms from England, our fashions from Paris, the patterns of our manufacturers from all parts of the world, and make nothing really original.'

Perkins deplored the lack of expertise available to consumers. He argued that you have jurists to make judgements about law, theologians to settle theological disputes, but matters of taste left him waving his hands in exasperation in the void. The effect of desperation was made worse by the awfulness of interiors in the 1890s: according to an article in the *Furnisher and Decorator*, the ordinary customer would rather weigh a piece of furniture than consider it aesthetically.

In her novel *The Custom of the Country* (1913) Edith Wharton describes a typical pre-de Wolfe interior:

> Mrs Spragg and her visitor were enthroned in two heavy gilt armchairs in one of the private drawing rooms of the Hotel Stentorian. The Spragg rooms were known as one of the Looey suites, and the drawing-room walls, above their wainscoting of highly varnished mahogany, were hung with salmon-pink damask and adorned with oval portraits of Marie Antoinette and the Princess de Lamballe. In the centre of the florid carpet a gilt table with a top of Mexican onyx sustained a palm in a gilt basket tied with a pink bow. But for this ornament, and a copy of *The Hound of the Baskervilles*, which lay beside it, the room showed no traces of human use, and Mrs Spragg herself wore as complete an air of detachment as if she had been a wax figure in a shop-window.

Into this cluttered vacuum rushed Elsie de Wolfe, the very woman who introduced new American money to old French furniture. At one brief meeting in 1913 Henry Clay Frick bought a reputed $3 million of French eighteenth-century furniture through Elsie de

Wolfe, who was paid 10 per cent commission as his adviser. A morning's work made her one of the richest independent women in New York and soon one of the most influential. Still today American collectors find it difficult to change the taste for French furniture implanted in the national psyche by de Wolfe's bravura shopping spree; even the fabulously wealthy Getty Museum (which could afford to collect anything) steadily and industriously accumulates eighteenth-century French furniture and little else.

In the furniture columns of women's magazines in the late nineteenth century we can see the beginnings of a popular neurosis, since methodically cultivated by the media. One contributor to the *Lady's Pictorial* answered letters privately for 7s 6d and would travel anywhere as a consultant on matters of taste for those suffering agonies of indecision for one guinea plus expenses. But Elsie de Wolfe brought it out of the closet. No longer anonymous, decoration became a branded commodity.

The chief, though never acknowledged, influence on Elsie de Wolfe was the book on interior design Edith Wharton wrote before her literary career really began. In 1897, at the age of thirty-five, Wharton published *The Decoration of Houses*. Her co-author was the architect Ogden Codman, also at the beginning of a career which in his case did not come to very much. With the Knickerbocker hauteur of one who could count Rhinelanders and Schermerhorns among her immediate ancestors, Wharton encouraged her readers – goaded by aspirational photographs of châteaux and palazzi – to dispose of the parlour sets and the Eastlake walnut and start all over again.

In *The Tastemakers* (1954) Russell Lynes described Elsie de Wolfe as:

A woman of gusto, quick temper, good figure and striking, but not pretty, appearance. She made a fetish of being unable to understand accounts and of always extracting from her business a whopping profit. She was sure of her tastes, all of which were expensive, and she was celebrated for standing on her head. She was an ardent devotee of callisthenics, raw vegetables and famous people, and if she was not the first woman decorator in America . . . she was certainly the first to turn her skill for the niceties of taste into a considerable fortune.

The Colony Club at 120 Madison Avenue (now the American Academy of Dramatic Arts) was her first major interior design commission, obtained through the intercession of the fashionable architect Stanford 'Stanny' White, junior partner of New York's McKim Mead and White, memorably described by Henry Adams in 1901 as the 'Moses, Aaron and Mahomet of the new rich'. De Wolfe's job of decorating White's 1905 design began with a voyage to England to buy Chippendale, mahogany candlestands, chimneypieces and chintz, so that the ladies of the club could relax in an environment that was bright, but also suggestive of old European money.

The club's governing committee initially found it too plain and barren, but were eventually won over by the elegant practicality of the 'Chintz Lady', who made frills and heavy drapes and antimacassars a thing of the past. The Colony Club, and in particular its widely imitated trellis room, made Elsie de Wolfe

Elsie de Wolfe, cheerful Sapphic decorator and popularizer of 'good taste'. Her aphorism: plenty of optimism and white paint!

famous, and the club's far-flung membership took word of her triumphs back to Palm Beach, San Francisco and Chicago.

A popular concept of 'good taste' was necessary to her proselytizing mission, which, with skilful marriages, exercise and a cheerful Sapphism became a lifetime's pastime. The term first appeared in her book *The House in Good Taste* (1915). (Ruskin and his contemporaries had discussed the opposite so much that 'bad taste' was a commonplace of popular journalism.) This book, together with her articles for the *Ladies' Home Journal* and other magazines, ushered into American homes a new form of dust-free brightness with the stirring motto, 'Plenty of optimism and white paint!'

The House in Good Taste was the climax of the attacks on 'bad taste', which was in fact the taste of the new middle classes for whom Thonet's elegant, inexpensive, mass-produced furniture promised so much. Mrs de Wolfe acquired a cultured persona on the flip side of ordinariness. She preferred the high places where she encouraged aesthetic defeatism, although her position relative to them was aspirational rather than occupational, as in Edith Wharton's case. She states her principles on page one: 'It is no longer possible, even to people of only faintly aesthetic tastes, to buy chairs merely to sit upon or a clock merely that it should tell the time. Home-makers are determined to have their houses, outside and in, correct according to the best standards.' And then, realizing she has travelled too far too fast: 'But what are the best standards? Certainly not those of the useless, overcharged house of the average American millionaire.'

The de Wolfe theory, if such a practical doctrine may be so named, skilfully combined intelligent respect for the past ('our ancestors knew what they were doing'), with diluted proto-modernism ('anything which works well, looks well'), and, most seductive of all to aspirational America, an anyone-can-do-it claim, perhaps intended as a slap in the face for the polite, but superior, Wharton caste: 'There never has been a house so bad that it couldn't be made over into something worthwhile.' This melded with a tempting introduction to creative self-expression: 'We must . . . visualize our homes . . . as individual expressions of ourselves.'

At her best Elsie de Wolfe spoke and decorated with refreshing clarity. Listen first to what the *Lady* of 1894 expected to find on a tabletop: 'a Dresden china candelabra, an old Worcester pot-pourri bowl, one delicate figure, a pair of old paste shoe buckles in a faded velvet case and an antique miniature'. Now Mrs de Wolfe: 'When you have emptied the tables of rubbish so that you can put things on them at need . . . your rooms will have meaning.'

Her terms of reference for the definition of taste were sham or authenticity, bringing to light, yet again, the flirtation of taste with morals. But the authenticity she sought was not necessarily to be found in antiques alone; no woman of quality should trifle with fakes, but Elsie de Wolfe was, like Viollet-le-duc, prepared to improve on the past if it was found wanting. She sounds very like the modern movement when she writes, 'We must learn to recognize suitability, simplicity and proportion, and apply our knowledge to our needs . . . We can exert our commonsense and decide whether a thing is suitable.'

The House in Good Taste was highly successful, going through numerous editions in the five years following publication. It was also influential; in 1926 John Wanamaker's store in Philadelphia even opened a department called 'Au Quatrième', where customers could have interior design counselling, and rival decorators set up in New York, including Ruby Ross Wood and Nancy McClelland, as well as abroad. In England Syrie Maugham and the aristocratic Sybil Colefax, driven into trade by the Crash of 1929, attracted particular attention, and for much the same reason: access to the press.

Elsie de Wolfe was one of the esoteric influences in the pages of American *Vogue* during the 1920s. She decorated the thirty-room apartment of its proprietor, Condé Nast, with crystal chandeliers, salmon-pink moiré curtains, Chien Lung wallpaper and mirrored cornices in a style that was characterized as enthusiastic French. For his daughter Natica's bedroom Elsie de Wolfe provided a design which was to be the first rebuff of her career and gave a sign of an imminent change in taste far more fundamental than the replacement of frills by *fauteuils*.

Natica Nast was a hard case. For her *boudoir* Elsie de Wolfe proposed more mirrored cornices, eggshell taffeta curtains, fruitwood *bergères*, Aubusson carpet and a dressing table that had come from Versailles. Natica instead specified a modern dressing table which she had custom-made at a Third Avenue furniture shop. An exchange, which included the deathless line, 'If it was good enough for Marie Antoinette it's good enough for you', did not prevent the rejection of the $10,000 piece.

Elsie de Wolfe did have a certain taste for simplicity and straightforwardness; in *Recipes for Successful Dining* (1934) she wrote, 'It is the humble dishes one comes back to with gusto and appreciation: the ragoût, grilled sole, roast chicken, risotto dishes in which all the ingredients are of the first quality . . . where each dish tastes like what it is and is innocent of yellow sauces and pink and black stars, beloved of second rate chefs.'

Her problem, if one can speak of so felicitous a life and career in such terms, was that she was unable to separate her theory of simplicity from her practice of laying on piles of glittering Looey with a trowel. Thus, dinner with Elsie might well be a humble grilled fish, but it was likely to be served by a butler on a gold lamé or *bourrette de soie* tablecloth, with bowls of white mennecy leaves filled with fruit and a centre-piece of salmon-coloured dahlias and zinnias with white Wedgwood china. You'd be lucky if you could even see the food.

The design of approved insurance

Just days after the 1929 Crash the Museum of Modern Art (MOMA) opened, offering a smarter European influence adapted for the Park Avenue palate. While modernism in Europe was perceived as an intellectual and creative revolution hand-made by Bolsheviks and whore-mongering, absinthe-soaked Bohemians, it was presented in Manhattan as a cleaned-up act, as if *Vogue* had styled the *bateau lavoir*, or as if Lord and Taylor ran the Bauhaus. The rich social moths attracted by the bright flame of modernism could scarcely be expected to identify with the political views

New York's Museum of Modern Art was a mausoleum for modern art. Its trenchant conservatism stimulated the observation that museums emerge only to cater for a subject when that subject is near to the end of its natural life.

of Picasso, even as they stashed away his can-vases. They would not understand the social theory of Walter Gropius (despite his own dedication to Fordism), even though they gazed admiringly at Henry-Russell Hitchcock's and Philip Johnson's seminal 1931 architecture exhibition at MOMA entitled the International Style.

When Gropius and his colleague Mies van der Rohe arrived from Germany, Tom Wolfe compared the scene to the stock movie recep-tion of white gods arriving in the jungle in a crashed plane. Although by no means as rad-ical as the name suggested, MOMA changed American taste. Modernism became high fashion rather than revolution. Gropius, the social engineer, would have worried more about this change of purpose had he not become a Harvard professor with a house in Lincoln, Massachusetts, while Mies became architectural adviser to corporate America.

Despite the sanitization of modernism, the elements of reform – so essential to its founders in Europe – remained inside the stylish cara-pace. MOMA's architecture and design depart-ment organized improving exhibitions, offering exemplary models of furniture to fill the vacuums of taste left when Elsie de Wolfe and all her Looeys were ousted.

In *The Personality of a House* (1931) Emily Post explains that modernism is just another style: 'Its personality should express your per-sonality, just as every gesture you make – or fail to make – expresses your gay ambition or your restraint, your old-fashioned conventions, your perplexing mystery, or your emancipated modernism – whichever characteristics are typically yours.'

In America, the application of modernism was a sort of approval insurance. In Britain, vestiges of social purpose clung to the sleek, speeding bandwagon. While Manhattan's Museum of Modern Art was a Narcissus pool for Knickerbocker social mountaineering using the art approach, Britain's Council for Indus-trial Design (COID) set about improving public taste.

In 1953 London's *Picture Post* ran a feature, the prototype of many to follow, showing two rooms decorated on the same budget, but to different effect. It reveals all the assumptions which the COID made about popular taste. They are like the beatitudes of popular modernism:

> The furniture trade says people buy what they like; 'designers' say they should learn to like something else.
> One room is cream (called 'dishonest yellow'); the other is white.
> One choice of furniture is clumsy, dowdy (but admittedly comfortable); the other is richly coloured and takes up less space.
> One carpet is easy to clean (or easy to keep dirty) Autumn Leaves; the other has off-white Indian rugs and kilims.
> One has a crow-step sand-tiled fireplace; the other is a spare rectangle with matt-black tiles framed in mahogany.
> One has high-shine dark oak; the other a swivel-topped table in cherrywood and elm, with white-spotted tobacco-brown upholstery.
> One bookcase is walnut with semi-circular glass doors; the other has open, adjust-able shelves.

One room has parchment shades on a central chandelier and a looming standard lamp; the other has articulated hanging lamps with Swedish red pleated shades and a plain metal desk lamp.

By such means were ghosts of Italian, German and Swedish modern designs smuggled into a few English homes, but never into country houses. Here taste remained doggedly reactionary. In Evelyn Waugh's parody *A Handful of Dust* (1934), Mrs Beaver (clearly a version of the decorator Syrie Maugham) violates a Victorian morning room with chrome furniture and sheepskin mats.

That the modern movement never had much real influence on popular taste in America or Britain is clear from a cursory examination of Nancy Reagan's White House and the Duchess of York's wedding list.

During President Reagan's first year in office his wife Nancy spent nearly $1 million on interior design, which caused rather a stir at a time of federal budget cuts. The work was done by Ted Graber, a decorator who reveals his nice sense of appropriateness in his preference for open-necked shirts in California and neckties when working on the East Coast. He was recommended to the Reagans by some of their show-business friends he had worked for in Beverly Hills.

The Graber style consists of new Looey Says coffee tables, lots of colour coordination, framed family photographs and hotel palms; Chinese wallpaper, chintz and the general pastel ambience in Nancy's quarters of expensive *nouvelle cuisine* restaurants. Elsie de Wolfe might have been back from the dead and work-

This comparative feature from *Picture Post* is an early expression of the view that the spiritual life of the nation could be spontaneously improved by access to Scandinavian furniture.

ing in Washington.

'Sister' Parish, the Queen of American decorating, who decorated the White House private
rooms during the Kennedy era, was commissioned to design the interiors of the Duke
and Duchess of York's new house at Sunninghill. Following the ancient tradition adopted by
the Reagans, newly married or new incumbents
have a strong and understandable desire to
style their environment. The extraordinary
thing here was that, while 'Sister' Parish and
her partner Albert Hadley have been recreating
throughout the United States a pseudo-English
style to please wealthy Connecticut matrons,
this very style of over-stuffed, fussy, antiqued
comfort has become so convincing an
expression of Englishness that now the royal
family wants it re-imported. In an interview
with the *Mail on Sunday* Parish explained that:
'Our point of view is based very simply on the
traditional values of quality, comfort, integrity
of design and appropriate furniture.'

The English royal family has a tradition of
redistributing heirlooms as wedding presents.
For their marriage in 1973 Princess Anne and
Captain Phillips received: a Chippendale desk
from Prince Philip, a butler's table and a chest
of drawers from the Duke of Gloucester, and
a nest of tables from Prince Andrew. This her-
metic, ritualized system tends to enforce a certain standard of taste by genetic drip. The context of all this real and imagined gentility,
whether on Capitol Hill or in Kensington
Palace, is the complete failure of modernism to
attract supporters other than fanatics. If you
insist on heirlooms as status symbols, or seize
on fake ones as caste marks, then it is inevitable
that you will require 'period' decoration. Faced

with a vacuum of taste, even presidents and
princes of the blood have recourse only to
hand-me-down interior design.

Decorators everywhere turn to the eighteenth century. David Hicks, who made a reputation in the 1950s for his daring use of colour,
including the juxtaposition of orange and
pink, skilfully reinterpreted eighteenth-century
design with its strong colours and geometric
patterns. At his own house in Britwell Salome,
Hicks achieved the desired 'mix' – you find
modern light fittings in Palladian rooms, as
well as the precious groupings of redundant
objects which he calls 'tablescapes'. In his book
On Living with Taste (1968) Hicks explains,
'I have been accused of being dogmatic; I am.
I would be useless to my clients if I were not.'

His estimation of his clients' opinions is clear
and the remark is as revealing of them as it is
of Hicks. Further on, he echoes Elsie de Wolfe:
'I have seen countless collections of incredibly
valuable furniture, pictures and objets d'art
where I longed to remove three quarters of the
contents and inject something simple and fresh
of today to give life and counterpoint to the
individually beautiful pieces.'

David Hicks achieved a distinctive style that
had some contemporary freshness, but not so
much as to embarrass the historical buildings
he usually worked in, to say nothing of the
arriviste clients he tended to work for. But,
compared with the dominant taste of the day,
the Hicks style appears to be almost revol-
utionary in its commitment to change.

The period since the Second World War, as
most of the foregoing suggests, has been one
of extraordinary nostalgia. Seeking value in a

restless age, people look backwards as if the stability afforded by the dead and their buried reputations can provide certainty. Few looked farther back than William Morris and, nowadays, he has crowds willing him back from the grave to send us all rushing headlong into a fake past. What Morris did not achieve in terms of turning the clock back himself, the guardians of his memory are doing in his name. To the decorator's repertoire established by Elsie de Wolfe and all her followers, Morris added cultural inertia. The net result was inertia in interior design. Passing fads became permanent. The prospect of development promised by Thonet's mass-production of furniture and so tentatively grasped by the modernists

David Hicks was the most original of that bastard tribe of interior 'decorators' who emerged in the 1950s. Hicks skilfully combined the artful clutter of the traditional country house with the fresh colours of European modern design.

was never realized.

The miserable tide-mark of Morris's influence is smeared across every revival, every stick of reproduction tat, every conservationist, every 'antique' (even the eighteenth-century ones). That his significance has been exaggerated does not matter, even if the chief exaggerator was the pioneer modernist historian, Nikolaus Pevsner. The subtitle of Pevsner's *Pioneers of the Modern Movement* (1936) – 'from William Morris to Walter Gropius' – suggests that the hairy stockbroker's son from Walthamstow was on the fast track to the twentieth century. Morris neither wanted nor deserved this role, but Pevsner misunderstood him because for a short while Morris's ideas about materials, techniques and morality seemed congruent with those of, say, Walter Gropius. To historians of Pevsner's bent the Whig interpretation of history was not to be questioned, and the mauve Victorian gloom of William Morris seemed necessarily to lead to a bright new century.

The English establishment did not take kindly to Morris being raised into the canon of modernism. John Betjeman took revenge on the German-Jewish scholar (whom he saw as a coarse materialist) by calling him 'Plebsveneer'. Pevsner wanted to believe that Morris was a visionary with a workable social theory that only needed streamlining through the use of new materials for it to be transferred to the Weimar Republic (and Gropius spoke of his debt to Morris), whereas Betjeman and his cronies just shared his nostalgia about the olden days.

This reaction is typically British. In certain quarters the view of Morris is still that he was

William Morris was both good and original: what was good was not original, and what was original was not good. He did have a certain touch as a designer of flat pattern, but otherwise was a melancholy influence on British design.

a thinker of monumental stature, a guardian of values that remain relevant. The truth, of course, is somewhat different. Morris is easy to write about, even if his vast corpus of ponderous prose and thudding, limping verse is difficult to read. An inevitable product of his education at Marlborough, with its coarse mishmash of wistful antiquarianism, he inspired C. P. Snow's bitterly perceptive observation that the greater part of English 'traditions' have their origin in the second half of the nineteenth century.

Morris is admired by enthusiasts who share his reluctance, even his inability, to come to terms with modern life; his hatred of contemporary civilization has been the most enduring part of his legacy. Although he was seventeen when the Great Exhibition opened in 1851 and therefore should have been old enough to understand Prince Albert's real purpose, he was not stimulated by industry, rather he recoiled from it. Unlike Albert, who saw the future as an indissoluble mixture of art and industry, Morris did not see the promise of technology, only the superficial dirt, only the divisions. Perhaps most importantly, he did not want to have his own life of wealth and privilege spoiled. He declared that 'we should do without coal' and revive the Middle Ages, an age where his various repressed fantasies could take form.

Although revivalism has been a recurrent influence in Western civilization, Morris's form of cultural regurgitation was different in that it was narrow, indulgent and sentimental. In his furniture he aped the vernacular. The books he published were not by modern authors, but by Chaucer. Not intended for an urban population hungry for education and delight, these were de luxe volumes for smug collectors, happy like Morris to be immersed in a selfish dream world.

Only in his paintings and graphic design did Morris achieve any originality. Morris's art was adolescent, but it had great power. With its gaudy eroticism, long-haired girls, constipated prose, bardic refrains, vegetarian colours, clumsy details and murky sensibilities he provided his narrow public with an irresistible mixture of sex and nostalgia, made safe by historical reference.

In 1814 Friedrich Koenig's high-speed printing press was first used on the London *Times*; in 1886 Werner von Siemens demonstrated his first self-excited generator; in 1883 Daimler and Maybach produced the high-speed petrol engine and in 1893 Rudolf Diesel unveiled his 'rational heat engine'. Morris's contribution to the century of progress was to found the Society for the Protection of Ancient Buildings, an organization which, as the prototype for all conservationist groups, was an important advance in the disease of nostalgia.

Sir Leslie Stephen once said, 'One thing is pretty certain; no one will ever want to revive the nineteenth century.' The influence of William Morris proved him wrong for, after the successful revival of the Georgians in the first half of the twentieth century, there was then enough historical space to revive the Victorians as well. In 1957, when the first effects of property speculation were being noticed in London, when new urban motorways were destroying their destinations, when Bunning's Coal Exchange had been made redundant by the post-war rationalization of the industry, Anne

John Betjeman, poetaster, professional snob and voice of a divided nation. While modern architecture was an exclusive import he admired it; when it threatened social engineering he repudiated it. Betjeman's achievement was to turn English complacency and slovenliness into a minor artform.

Countess of Rosse (wife of the founder of the Georgian Group) gave a party in her home in Stafford Terrace (which once belonged to *Punch* illustrator Linley Sambourne) in order to launch a society dedicated to reviving the nineteenth century. There were blood-lines all over the place. Among those present at the founding of the Victorian Society three months later were the decorator John Fowler and the poet John Betjeman.

Although, according to Evelyn Waugh, Betjeman was a mere schoolboy doing brass rubbings while Harold Acton was trying to revive the Victorian era during the 1920s, it was Betjeman's popularity as a public figure that helped make nostalgia so much a cult in contemporary Britain. While he poured scorn on most late-twentieth-century inventions, Betjeman was not prepared to disdain television in promulgating his aesthetic faith. Strange to say, in Betjeman we can trace the curious path of modernism in British life and culture.

Betjeman was attracted to modernism because its first spokesman in Britain was an aesthete educated at Eton and King's College, Cambridge called Philip Morton Shand, a friend of Le Corbusier and Aalto and translator of Gropius. From so sophisticated and cosmopolitan a source, modernism seemed exciting and even élitist. *Ghastly Good Taste* (1933) in fact ends in praise of the Bauhaus, but this was an eclectic age when the *Architectural Review* published Georgian details alongside articles championing heliotherapy in international-style Swiss sanatoria, Canadian grain silos and Soviet gymnasia.

Indeed, for as long as modernism was not

a social threat, the English eclectic tradition encouraged it as an exotic creature. But as soon as it ceased to be a diversion for dilettantes, Betjeman and his followers dropped it like a proverbial hot cake. The Second World War was the turning point: just as Evelyn Waugh was moved to write his saccharine and sentimental novel *Brideshead Revisited* in response to the material and spiritual privations of 1939–45, so too James Richards, editor of the *Architectural Review* (for whom Betjeman was then working), was stimulated to write in 1946 a plausible, if rather sickly, panegyric about the suburbs. The title, *The Castles on the Ground*, alludes to what is usually said about the Englishman's home.

But Shand also became disaffected with modernism and took up the cultivation of endangered apples instead. His last thoughts about modern architecture were expressed in a letter to Betjeman which he wrote shortly before his death in 1960: 'I am haunted by a gnawing sense of guilt in having, in however minor and obscure degree, helped to bring about . . . a monster neither of us could have foreseen.'

To Betjeman and his circle architecture was a pursuit comparable to bird-watching, having nothing to do with social purpose (except of a very conservative sort) and thus his artistic eclecticism and social snobbery soon got the upper hand of his febrile flirtation with the buildings of socialist realism. Betjeman was happiest when safe in a world of trains and buttered toast. He was always a conservationist, his dream-world doggerel was written to memorialize a genteel vision of a country which never really existed – except in the poet's

imagination. He feared an 'England . . . all council houses and trunk roads and steel and glass factory blocks',[10] and now with the Victorian Society there was a society to help him fantasize. It is true that Nikolaus Pevsner too had been in at the founding of the Victorian Society, but the great professor played a part because at first it seemed that any organization dedicated to architecture must be admirable. What Pevsner really wanted was a Forschungs Institut; what he got was a reactionary clique.

Betjeman never wrote a serious book about architecture, but in his quirky television presentations he became its popular champion. He never wrote a decent poem, but became poet laureate. An apostate of modernism, anti-intellectual, anti-serious, anti-semitic and antiquarian, John Betjeman was a quaint schoolmaster type who raised trivia to the status of a great national pursuit. He was the perfect topographer of the English soul. But the price of his persuasive, if rather smug and smarmy, vision of all the nice things in the world – by which he meant brown garden walls, silvery frosty Sunday nights, a view of St Botolph's, a cup of tea, a sunny afternoon, a snooze, cigarettes and comfy chairs – was the loss of a positive view of the future which might be different to the cosy version of the past.

Betjeman defined and captured a certain middlebrow taste in Britain. His personal achievement at vicarage tea parties neatly complemented that of the National Trust at a national level. Only since 1945 has the National Trust been concerned with the preservation of houses. Originally its founders – Octavia Hill, Robert Hunter and Canon

The breakfast room at Nostell Priory was typical of the restorative work undertaken by the National Trust, inventing a past for a new population which had never really had one.

Rawnsley – sought to preserve the countryside and coastline; its aim was to keep vile industry away and, more sensibly, in Octavia Hill's words 'to provide open-air sitting rooms for the poor'.

The change in character of the National Trust from an amenity society to an antiquarian cult was, like so much else in modern Britain, made possible by the new tax structures imposed after the end of the First World War. The second National Trust Act of 1937, passed after years of lobbying by Lords Lothian and Zetland, allowed the owners of country houses to transfer their property and land to the National Trust, which, being a charity, did not have to pay taxes on them. The Trust would maintain historic buildings in perpetuity, while the owner's family continued to live in the property in exchange for agreeing to open it to the common people. Thus was the habit of visiting country houses born and a version of interior design based on an artificial reverence for the past was made public.

Under the administration of James Lees-Milne, the trust soon acquired a handsome portfolio of historic property: among the first were Blickling Hall, Cliveden, Polesden Lacey, Lacock, West Wycombe and Speke Hall. Many more were to follow and in this way a particular vision of Britain's heritage was imposed on popular taste.

The National Trust country-house scheme set out to prove the assumption in Evelyn Waugh's comic novels that the past is always better. Each reveals a total disdain for theory, a distrust of the modern world. Waugh, who was born above a dairy in North London, even set himself up in his country house Combe Florey, a case of life imitating art.

John Fowler was a furniture salesman from Peter Jones who collaborated with Sybil Colefax to create an influential firm of decorators. Fowler's style was an eclectic one.

After the Second World War country-house owners, who had mostly had their properties requisitioned between 1939 and 1945, had the opportunity to rethink the demands of the interior. They rethought and came to the same conclusions. John Fowler created the post-war country house interior very much according to principles of his own invention, and this became National Trust taste. His style of 'humble elegance' did not come cheap, particularly when his fastidious taste required sixteen different shades of white on one ceiling or the lowering of an entire cornice by two inches to improve the proportions of a room.

Fowler's expensive shabby chic fixed a certain image of the 'quality' English interior. David Mlinaric replaced Fowler as the dominating influence on the National Trust and with this change historical accuracy replaced intuitive pastiche, a sign of professionalism that matched the ever increasing status of the country house.

Yet some architects and designers who believe that the only responsible path is to explore contemporary possibilities have rebelled against this. As early as 1904 Norman Shaw would have none of it. In his essay in *The British Home Today* he complained,

> The present day belief that good design consists of pattern — pattern repeated ad nauseam — is an outrage on good taste. A wallpaper should be a background pure and simple — that, and nothing else. The art teaching of today follows in the steps of William Morris, a great man who somehow delighted in glaring wallpapers. The kind of paper hanging that we need most of all is

The elements of John Fowler's aesthetic: a stripped-down and highly selective antiquarianism which was highly original.

what I may describe ... as the 'tone' wallpaper.

The aesthetic of a designer such as Dieter Rams – 'To me good design means as little design as possible' – derives from the declarations of humility taught by the Fathers of the Church. That less is more does not have to mean austere reductivism. In the modern world, with all its vulgar surplus and clutter, it represents a challenge which has as its objective not bland utilitarianism, but the thrill of refined, sensuous pleasure. It is far more difficult to make things easy than complicated. Mystification is simple; clarity is more demanding.

David Mlinaric inherited John Fowler's reputation. His fussy, fastidious and scholarly interior restorations and reconstructions were a powerful influence on taste.

More is not only a bore, it runs against the strongest continuous element in European culture: a belief in progress validated by the fragile vision of perfectibility. The Thonet chair offered an idea of industrialized perfectibility, but in Britain and the United States the consumers with discretionary income preferred the heraldry of real or bogus pedigree.

Interior design is a business whose substance is a subterfuge; it derives its character from historical ignorance and its status from social fear. If the example of Thonet had been accepted, if there were more beautiful everyday things in the shops for fastidious people to buy, interior designers would be out of work. These pimps of taste flourish in the red light district of culture.

Terence Conran's flat in Fitzrovia, c.1966. A masterful, not to say opportunistic, combination of English vernacular with continental chic which inspired shops and magazine spreads for nearly a quarter of a century.

Laura Ashley's great skill was to identify a fragment of English provincial taste and turn it into a commercial phenomenon.

André Putnam's monochrome pastiches of modernist masterpieces were designed to be photographed rather than lived in.

FASHION

Being and Dressing

No one has ever taken very seriously the proposition that we are what we wear, but there is no doubt that we want it to appear to be so. At the height of the Depression, with shoeless waifs littering the streets of every major city, banking in chaos and manufacturing in decline, a Bohemian immigrant girl was reported saying, 'After all, life is mostly what you wear', an apophthegm whose source, content and message nicely emphasize the richly charged language of clothes.[11]

When it comes to the meaning of things, there are no more powerful transmitters than clothes, those quasi-functional devices which, like an inverted fig, put the heart of the matter in front of the skin. Ralph Lauren, whose business it has been to turn chain-store clothing into heraldry, said in an interview with *New York* magazine in 1985, 'Clothing sets your taste; it's your outward expression, it's the first shot, it's what you say about yourself to the world.' But judging by appearances – a practice popularized but not originated by Oscar Wilde – exposes the contradiction that is central to fashion. Nothing is as crass and vulgar as instant classification according to hairstyle, clothing and footwear, yet it is an irresistible temptation and a cruelly accurate analytical form. In literature, from Laurence Sterne to Evelyn Waugh to Tom Wolfe, a sort of inheritor of an English satirical tradition, clothes are used to express character. In *The Bonfire of the Vanities* (1988) Wolfe assassinates all his characters with remorseless and sesquipedalian descriptions of what they are wearing: there is a professor in 'rotting tweeds' and all the black muggers wear Reebok trainers. Thus tweeds and trainers, to say nothing

Fashion: Being and Dressing   143

of their wearers, are categorized. That some critics have described Wolfe's laundry list technique as malicious reveals its deadly accuracy in betraying taste and motivation.

Even in subsistence economies people rarely dress simply to avoid being naked. We think of our clothes as we think of our bodies: more so than other possessions, they are an extension of our self. We are grateful for any praise they excite and are dismayed if they cause disdain or indifference.

Clothes are a sort of theatre where the leading player – the self – is torn between function and decoration, protection and assertion, concealment and display. This everyday drama reinforces the idea that clothes have a social and cultural function and as such are vital evidence in the study of aesthetic preference: what you wear is a matter of taste. And so, of course, is what you refuse to wear. Clothes have always been held to be the most explicit confessions of status, or distinction through decoration. That's why we know a Tom Wolfe hero is bound for a fall when we read he's wearing hand-made shoes and an $1,800 suit. Equally, although perhaps less understandably, a man is morally suspect if his wife buys his trousers.

Clothes are so inflammatory that injunctions have existed since antiquity to moderate the power of dress to upset the *status quo*: there is a sort of politics to fashion. The width of the purple border on a Roman senator's toga was wider than on a Roman knight's. Dress codes flourished towards the end of the Middle Ages as a means of buttressing the existing social estates at a time when the feudal nobility felt threatened by the emerging bourgeoisie, a class becoming increasingly able to articulate

The Theory of the Leisure Class

'No one finds difficulty assenting to the commonplace that the greater part of the expenditure incurred by all classes for apparel is incurred for the sake of respectable appearance rather than for the protection of the person. And probably at no other point is the sense of shabbiness so keenly felt as it is if we fall short of the standard set by social usage in this matter of dress . . . People will undergo a very considerable degree of privation in the comforts or necessaries of life in order to afford what is considered *a decent amount of wasteful consumption*; so that it is by no means an uncommon occurrence, in an inclement climate, for people to go ill clad in order to appear well dressed . . . The need of dress is eminently a "higher" or spiritual need.'

Thorstein Veblen, *The Theory of the Leisure Class*, 1904

Trainers were adopted by people who would risk colonic rupture if they broke into a run. Details such as the length of the tongue became caste marks.

'This man, lady, hath robbed many hearts of their particular additions; he is valiant as the lion, churlish as the bear, slow as the elephant: a man into whom nature hath so crowded humours that his valour is crushed into folly.' *Troilus and Cressida*

its position by visual means (and nowadays dedicated to the practice). Ostentatious dress was repeatedly cited as a characteristic of the worldly city life (think of the strictures of Savonarola) and met with disapproval from austere churchmen. Of course, the considerable increase in ordinances on the subject of immodest dress in the early modern period suggests a concomitant increase in their violation.

In Renaissance Italy officials upbraided citizens for wearing ermine instead of sackcloth, buttons instead of studs. Such regulations in matters of taste were intended to enforce authority during periods of social change. The problem of sustaining rank was especially acute in England during the reign of Elizabeth I, who in 1597 passed a decree limiting silk embroidery and the general use of velvet to women who were married to knights, or above – the equivalent today of designer labels being restricted by statute to the wives of senior management. The vested interests of those most concerned to preserve the visible distinctions of class are described in Philip Stubbes's *The Anatomie of Abuses* (1583). On the one hand he cautioned against 'the pride of apparell', which he felt was a cause of wickedness and sin, while on the other he argued for strict demarcations in dress so that one class would have its authority over another reinforced by visual means.

Sumptuary laws expose the intimate bond between clothes and social competition, the conspicuously dressed *arriviste* always being a threat to the establishment. Imitation and emulation, the driving forces in fashion, compelled first the aristocracy and then the bourgeoisie to resort to increasingly elaborate devices to maintain the differentials upon which a comfortable and familiar social order depends. In those most conservative callings, the law, church and universities, ancient dress codes are frozen and the requirement still exists to exert authority by symbolic means.

There is now a free market in the consumption of clothes: an actress dresses as sumptuously as a princess and self-made businessmen can purchase a version of respectability at outfitters who once specialized in cladding gentlefolk. The messages about clothing are less clear, but not less significant. The first person to distance himself from this primal phenomenon in modern consumerism and report on it was Thorstein Veblen, whose celebrated dissection of the 'pecuniary canons of taste' neatly described how clothes operate as signals of wealth and lifestyle. His famous expression 'conspicuous consumption' explained the impulse to astonish and impress through costly ornaments. Inspired by sartorial devices such as slashing in order to reveal gorgeous undergarments, Veblen went on to explain that purchasing power is a crude but effective measure of sumptuousness and therefore of *intention*.

Teasing exhibitionism can be dramatic, but redundancy is a more subtle and effective means of communicating authority: clothes which inhibit physical exertion such as high-heeled shoes denote status because they suggest a privileged life of selective idleness. Similarly, clothes made of astonishingly impractical materials such as linen, silk and cashmere powerfully demonstrate a hauteur about maintenance and depreciation in the wardrobe. In cultures with different values, easy-care fabrics would quite properly be considered luxurious.

But the functionally redundant high-heeled shoe is more than a symbol of feminine inertia; it is, as Freud knew, a powerful sexual fetish. The *Tatler* reported David Bailey as saying, 'I like high heels – I know it's chauvinistic. It means girls can't run away from me.' This characteristic of high-heeled shoes has in itself made them victims of inertia in the fast moving world of fashion. They are enduringly erotic. To find out why, you should perhaps think first of flat shoes. Summon up an image of an espadrille: salt-bleached, unravelling rope sole, rucked down at heel. The woman wearing it has a mid-calf denim skirt, a T-shirt and beads, a big, loose and toothy grin and straw blonde hair, greying slightly. Swedish. Very nice in its way, but the style is domestic and maternal, fundamentally practical.

It is the flagrant lack of practicality that makes high-heeled shoes so fascinating: in terms of static mechanics they induce a sort of insecurity which some find titillating. If a woman wears a high-heeled shoe it changes the apparent musculature of the leg so that you get an effect of twanging sinew, of tension needing to be released. Her bottom sticks out like an offering. At the same time, the lofty perch is an expression of vulnerability, she is effectively hobbled and unable to escape. There is something arousing about this declaration that she is prepared to sacrifice function for form. A glossy finish enhances the effect: there is simply no knowing what a girl who offers herself in this way wouldn't do in pursuit of superficial pleasure.

Ultimately, it is the ironic tension between form and function and material which gives the high heel shoe its meaning. It's the same

with a silk brassière. The chosen material is so at odds with the task in hand: vacuum-bonded honeycomb composite would be a more effective way of containing the brave vibration of a bust. A silk bra shows you don't care and that you are a slave to appearances and to the senses: slavery, sense and appearance – the three sum up high-heel shoes and, indeed, the erotic element in clothing.

Ever since a woman first wore a waist string, the protective function of clothing has been secondary to its ornamental purpose. A waist string holding up a kind of small apron front and rear draws yet more attention to the sexual parts, and hence is an extension rather than a diminution of the original erotic purpose. Even in cold climates, coloured body drawings,

The high heel is the most obvious expression of a sensual disdain for function in dress: a dedication to effect rather than use suggests a sensitive interest in pleasure which is highly erotic.

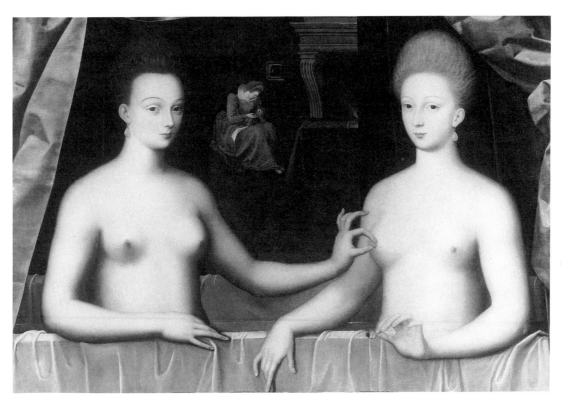

which have no thermal advantage against the weather, were evidently as highly regarded as clothes of more obviously functional character. Until relatively recently Australian aborigines only wore decorative ornaments and went quite naked even in the coldest weather, preferring to clasp a glowing log for warmth. In Tasmania, the aborigines choose to relax by standing on one foot, further proof – if proof were needed – that contemporary European attitudes to comfort and to function are themselves mere matters of preference – of taste.

The very notion of 'modesty' in dress is culturally specific and when probed reveals a deep ambivalence, rooted in its correlation with desire. In a 1985 interview with *Fortune* magazine, Leslie Wexner, founder of The Limited,

In matters of fashion sixteenth-century plunging necklines often left breasts entirely exposed, removing attention from the codpiece and creating a demand for a new range of gestures.

Concealment and display are two of the chief devices of eroticism, although pornography knows no such subtlety. Its fascination is anthropological rather than sexual.

quoted, with evident approval, Charles Revson's beguiling little nostrum, 'Women all hope they get laid.' Later, developing his theme for *New York* magazine in 1987, he declared, 'Uptight women stockbrokers will put on a G-string when they get home.'

If the ostensible aim of modesty is to combat desire, the effect is often the opposite, as the frequency of nun imagery in pornography suggests. Concealment stimulates the imagination to a degree that exposure cannot hope to emulate. This game between prudery and style is a stimulus to fashion and fashion is nothing more than clothing at work in the marketplace.

As the sexuality of the female body is more diffused than the male's, exposure of one part customarily concealed helps focus attention. *Décolletage* first appeared during the fifteenth century and since then the emphasis of fashion has shifted from one erogenous zone to another. Taking a synoptic look at fashion, men appear to be able to absorb only one zone at a time, rather as it is said to be impossible to feel pain in two places simultaneously. Thus, fashion draws attention first to this and then to that, whether by exposing, concealing, emphasizing, exaggerating or distorting.

The varying threshold of embarrassment and the moveable limits of modesty characterize civilization in its erratic progress. During the Middle Ages indignation could be aroused by the wearing of pointed shoes, whose symbolism was made more explicit by the attachment of a phallus to one foot (perhaps an unconscious expression of the idea, untested by science and all the stronger for it, that the foot and the penis are related in terms of size, if not function). Similarly, when plunging necklines of the sixteenth century left breasts completely exposed, codpieces became less pronounced.

Like all forms of behaviour, manners in dress started as innovative fashions and through custom evolved to become a part of the social repertoire. Wherever codes govern dress, the partnership of taboo and desire lurks concealed. Modesty, we have seen, is simply a matter of taste. It is not natural and is meaningless outside a specific cultural context. Indian women were once shocked by Western women wearing hats, a practice felt to be a male prerogative. In seventeenth-century Massachusetts dress was part of a morality of taste inspired by a religion which abhorred ceremony, ritual and delight. It was, after all, said of the Puritans that they condemned bear-baiting not so much because it caused misery for the bear but more because it gave pleasure to the audience. Puritan clothes were designed to separate individuals from their own bodies, to say nothing of the bodies of others. Not for the first time these regulations had their origin in notions of modesty which benefited the ruling class or caste. While taboos restrict conscious behaviour, they stimulate desire in the unconscious. Today, fashion thrives on a similarly ambivalent relationship between convention and outrage.

The status of artists, beauty itself, female desirability and even posture and gait are aesthetic preferences, rather than absolutes. Even sickness and health are influenced by fashion, which, in turn, is influenced by fashionable disorders. The early Victorian enthusiasm for romantic melancholy – think of Mendelssohn's 'Frei aber Einsam' sonata – produced widespread and modish invalidism. Extraordinary numbers of young people went into decline and died before maturity, a particularly ironic case of life imitating art.

Tight lacing may or may not have been a predisposing cause, but women were certainly prepared to go to peculiar lengths to achieve a fashionable appearance of delicacy and fragility. Drinking vinegar and reading all night were known to achieve the desired pallor and the longed-for rings under eyes whose pupils were often dilated by belladonna. Gustave Flaubert's account of his sister's wake is shocking evidence of this taste for implied and real putrefaction.[12] At about the same time such fashionable ladies as there were in La Corrèze in France crowded into Tulle's courtroom to experience the stench from Lafarge's guts after his execution. For a moment in the nineteenth century, the world *à la mode* acted as if it had been briefly reprieved from the grave and was about to return to it.

The Romantic preference for yellow makeup and other manifestations of putridity was a reaction to the aristocratic Restoration taste for pink and white facial designs. Lady Wishfort in William Congreve's *The Way of the World* (1700) had 'cracks discernible in the white vernish'. This aesthetic was influenced by the rose and the lily, the flowers of chivalry, which had medieval origins. During the late Middle Ages cosmetics began to appear in court circles and the quality of looking glasses improved. For the first time since Imperial Rome, portraiture was revived, although, curiously, fashions in cosmetics soon drove the female – not long released from the veil – back into the anonymity of the stereotype.

It is a measure of the power of art over nature that we now perceive the invented formula of pink and white faces to be 'natural'. The first Queen Elizabeth was addicted to ceruse, a compound of white lead and vinegar used to maintain virginal whiteness. Freckles were eradicated by sublimates of mercury. In pursuit of an ideal her majesty's contemporaries might use Spanish hair pads, false hips, steel busks, panniers and high heels. In so manipulating human form subjects were vulnerable to the charge of practising witchcraft.

After the eccentricities of later Romanticism, cosmetics were not used by respectable women until the twentieth century. Pompadour's marmoreal complexion had already contributed to the middle-class notion that it was aristocratic to be white and the extraordinary cult of elegant cleanliness, described by Etienne Tourtelle in his *Eléments d'hygiene* (1797) and the Comtesse de Bradi in her *Du savoir en France au 19ème siècle* (1858).

Public hygiene was the exercise in favour of the olfactory sense that lessons in taste, from Henry Cole and others, were to the visual. Just as persuading the workers to wash was believed to enhance their wisdom, so persuading them to prefer one sort of design was expected to do the same. Both are expressions of the values being forged for the middle classes in the various workshops of the world. The taste developed for cleansing the skin, rather than disguising it, and the pores were to be aired rather than clogged (but bathing itself was to be treated with caution).[13]

In the twentieth century another form of facial coloration inspired by confused ideas of healthfulness, the suntan, became fashionable.

States of health are as much matters of taste as of medical science. It was once fashionable for young women to cultivate the look that Swinburne described as 'death taken seasick'.

In his *Maxims of Piety and Christianity* Thomas Wilson wrote, 'All such dresses are forbidden which incite irregular desires.'

Although related to the Victorian vogue for sea-bathing, the idea that tanned skin is attractive goes back no further than the 1920s, when pseudo-scientific theories of heliotherapy were developed by mad doctors in Swiss and German clinics. Heliotherapy went hand in hand with nudism, modernist tea parties, the international style in architecture and youth movements. Coco Chanel made the suntan chic, which elevated it from a ragbag of crypto-fascist ideas to a high fashion statement. Evelyn Waugh's Gilbert Pinfold hated suntans as much as he despised Picasso, plastic and jazz.

Although the 'Côte d'Azur' was christened by an obscure Burgundian poet, Stephen Liege-ard (after his birthplace, the Côte d'Or), the English made it a tourist destination. Lord Brougham was trapped in Cannes during the cholera outbreak of 1834 and acquired a liking for the area. Soon taken up by the fashionable,

the Riviera's English patrimony is commemor-
ated in the local names: Promenade des Ang-
lais, Hôtel Carlton, l'avenue du Capitaine
Scott. The cult of the Mediterranean and its
luscious brown skins burst over Britain with
special force in the 1950s, when D. H. Lawrence's books with their frequent Mediterranean focus were becoming popular.

Intellectual monthlies such as *Encounter*
often contained articles by latter-day Byrons,
their skin the colour of a nicotine stain.
Languishing in Ibiza or Capri, as they struggled
to finish yet another fifteen-shilling novel, they
mused wistfully about the beatniks on the
ferry. The image was given extra force by
Brigitte Bardot, whose first film, *Et Dieu créa
la femme* (1956) vindicated not only her savage

By the 1930s exciting irregular desires was a stock-in-
trade of fashion clothing and behavioural cults. The
heliophilia of the 1930s was based on cranky medical
theories which gained popularity when colour film
and cheap travel made explicit the link between
suntans and stars.

Right Paul Poiré described Coco Chanel's elegantly restrained style as '*misérablisme de luxe*'.

Below The Carlton Hotel, Nice. The entire Côte d'Azur, from Menton to Hyères, was an invention of British travellers, as the legacy of local names suggests.

potency as a symbol of amoral sexuality, but also the attractiveness of suntans.

The questionable benefits to health of permanently tanned skin were successfully promoted and reinforced by films and advertisements, to say nothing of the perennial nut-brown President Kennedy. A tanned complexion is still read as an unmistakable sign of youth and vitality, and even the proletarianization of Mediterranean travel has failed to diminish the allure of the tan. One hundred years ago it would have been considered impolite, two hundred years ago, repulsive. Edward Gibbon was fat, pale and proud of it. We are too conditioned in regarding prevailing conventions as necessarily desirable to recognize them as products of taste not of science.

Fashion is primitive in its insistence on exhi-

Roger Vadim's movie *Et Dieu créa la femme* packaged sun and sand (the Côte d'Azur) with sex (Brigitte Bardot); blondes and St Tropez became famous.

A holiday in the sun may be cheaper than staying at home, but the suntan still has massive allure in terms of body heraldry.

bitionism, which withers in isolation. The catwalk fashion show with its incandescent hype is its apotheosis. A ritualized gathering of connoisseurs and the spoilt at a spotlit parade of snazzy pulchritude, it is an industrialized version of the pagan festivals of renewal. At the end of each seasonal display, a priesthood is enjoined to carry news of the omens to the masses.

In his book *Système de la Mode* (1967), Roland Barthes showed how the rhetoric of fashion disguises the inherent contradiction of creating absolutes, only to discard them as *passé* after a predictable period of time has elapsed. The journalist or the copywriter blurs memories of the immediate past by discrediting the language which justified last season's style, while simultaneously embracing this year's models with euphoric enthusiasm.

Fashion is the most intense expression of the phenomenon of neomania, which has grown ever since the birth of capitalism. Neomania assumes that purchasing the new is the same as acquiring value. Adopting bogus algebraic formulae to dissect the tropes of the fashion writer's prose, Barthes describes the role of accelerators whose task it is to sustain fashion by precipitating the renewal of clothing. If the purchase of a new garment coincides with the wearing out of an old one, then obviously there is no fashion. If a garment is worn beyond the moment of its natural replacement, there is pauperization. Fashion flourishes on surplus, when someone buys more than he or she needs. In the motor industry this was known as planned obsolescence, or, more charitably, the dynamic economy. The more the rhythm of purchase dominates the rhythm of dilapidation, the stronger the submission to fashionable tastes.

Magazines suggest that fashion thrives on confusion and arbitrary change; their rhetoric is highly stylized, a selectively gushing narrative which defines its role in the market-place. But if fashion is unpredictable and anarchic up close, it appears more regular from afar – distance lends order to the view. Women's fashions are subject to long-term cyclical variation, and by measuring certain parameters such as the width of the waist over a century it can be shown that major oscillations in fashion occur at a rate of about once a century, although perhaps with increasing frequency.

This observation was irresistibly attractive to determinists wanting to reconcile the great tides of history with the little eddies of fashion. Thus, it has been said that France, from just before the Revolution to the aftermath of the Napoleonic Wars, saw agitations in the wardrobe as complete and exciting as those on the national stage. Similarly, the peaceful and prosperous reign of Queen Victoria witnessed decades of subfusc tranquillity in dress.

The *bals publics* of the *Directoire* period offer tempting evidence that vast generic causes in history do in fact have minute specific effects. Emancipated Parisians celebrated their survival and their freedom at the Bal des Victoires in the Hôtel Richelieu. They dressed for the party by cutting their hair short at the nape of the neck as if in preparation for the guillotine and they wore a thin red ribbon as if to indicate the cut of the blade. Friends were greeted with a sharp movement of the head, in imitation of the victim's spasm under the knife. Modelled on Aspasia, dancers with naked arms and breasts wore transparent draperies below which, it was said, would scarcely further offend prudes if they were removed in their entirety.

No doubt there was an element of relief in this licentious display, but it is ironical that the austere neo-classical standards of the Revolution only achieved form when the ideals of Republican virtue had given way to a great deal of shameless hedonism. Attempts at imitating classical civilization by aping classical dress were fascinating, but not contagious. The same spirit fired *les Barbus*, bearded classicizing men contemporary with the beautiful, patrician paintings of Jacques-Louis David, but with less to offer history. The failure of these particular experiments in dress inspired leaders of fashion

Neoclassical evening dress from Ackermann's
Repository of Arts.

to seek democratic models that were nearer home in terms of both time and space.

English liberty and therefore English fashion were soon considered worthy of emulation. The early decline of the influence of the court in English life had a profound effect on life and manners, particularly as compared to the French. While sun kings radiated and courtiers sunbathed, decentralized English society encouraged the cult of the independent amateur. The idle periwigs and indulgent rouge of the courtier contrasted with the stout boots and the coarse cloth of the country gentleman. Functional influences created new styles which soon became stereotypes: the English country gentleman cut away the skirts at the front of his jacket to make it easier to mount and ride a horse. Crowns of hats rose to provide surer protection against falls. The button-down collar reflects the polo player's requirement that his collar does not flap in his face. No areas of human activity have shaped fashion so much as sport and 'politics'.

The end of the Terror in France allowed *émigrés* to return and they brought with them a taste for English modes and manners. As the final flourish of eighteenth-century artificiality died, a new cult of the dandy emerged. Dandyism was not a style, but an attitude, based on early attempts to codify the modern phenomenon of the 'gentleman'. Beau Brummel, despite his personal notoriety, emphasized that the essence of dandyism was not to be conspicuous. Lord Chesterfield wrote in 1745, 'Dress is a very foolish thing; and yet it is a very foolish thing for a man not to be well-dressed.'

Dandies developed this notion into a

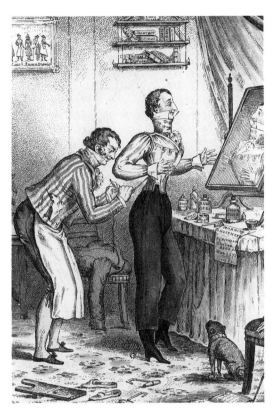

Dandies misunderstood. The matter of success in being and dressing must be nicely judged. Lord Chesterfield wrote to his son, 'Never be the first or the last in fashion.'

language of objects, regarding dress as an exquisite means of expressing an assumed superiority of character. Thus the dandy played an important part in defining modern consciousness – we are all nowadays, to an extent, dandies. Charles Baudelaire noted in 1836, 'Dandyism appears especially in transitory periods when democracy is not yet all powerful, and when aristocracy is only partially unsettled and depreciated . . . Dandyism is a setting sun; like the star in its decline, it is superb, without heat and full of melancholy.'

Dandyism was an episode in the development of middle-class taste and while, as Baudelaire realized, in cult terms it was historically specific, it donated something to the emerging bourgeois personality that seems to be ineradicable. By the late nineteenth century the dandy had developed into something extreme, characterized by more than just an attitude to clothes. Oscar Wilde epitomized it, and was described by George Macmillan as 'aesthetic to the last degree, passionately fond of secondary colours, low tones, Morris papers, and capable of talking a good deal of nonsense thereupon, but for all that a very sensible, well-informed and charming man.'[14]

Wilde's dandyism was, of course, a form of revenge on the bourgeoisie. Far from presaging a classless society, the decline of old aristocratic mores gave rise to yet more intricate codes of behaviour – this time restricted to and developed by the middle classes. Simplicity and appropriateness were the guiding principles of a doctrine which clothed the middle-class male in a variety of uniforms. In a conformist age the only available distinction was the subtle one of the cut of a good tailor. The creation

of the well-dressed English 'gentleman' was a
device to carry the burden of a nation translat-
ing itself from centuries of conquering into a
future of trading and decline.[15]

The style of the gentleman spread, with the
British Empire, across the world. Even in the
tropics black silk hats and frock coats were
aped. In Vienna at the turn of the century a
curious mix of Anglophilia and incipient modernism produced an intense admiration for the
English gentleman's wardrobe, as if John Buch-
an's Richard Hannay had read Freud. No
aspect of daily life was too banal for Adolf
Loos's system of aesthetics: to him, good manners in dress, as in architecture and design,
depended on the absence of ornament and
functional appropriateness. In *Das Andere*
(*The Outsider*), published in 1903, Loos
attempted, among the aromatic vapours of
Viennese decadence, a systematic analysis of
everyday life. Loos execrated ornament with
all the vigour that Freud had shown in exclud-
ing from his own vision of the soul every device
that the nineteenth century had used to camouflage its primitive mechanisms.

Like the doyennes of American interior
decoration, in the first edition Loos even
undertook to answer readers' enquiries on the
subject of dress.

> How should one dress? Fashionably. When
> is one fashionably dressed? When you draw
> least attention to yourself. I do not draw
> attention to myself. I travel to Timbuctoo
> or Kratzenkirchen. There everybody stares
> at me. Because there I draw attention to
> myself. A great deal. So I have to make a
> modification. You are fashionably dressed

By the second half of the nineteenth century – the
period when, according to C. P. Snow, most British
'traditions' were established – gentlemen's dress
codes had become a means of imposing order on
turbulent society.

when you do not draw attention to yourself in the centre of Western culture on a particular occasion. It is afternoon and I am happy that I do not draw attention to myself in my grey striped trousers, my frock-coat and my top hat. I stroll about Hyde Park. Stroll about and suddenly find myself in Whitechapel. And again I draw a great deal of attention to myself. I must make another modification. You are only fashionably dressed, when in the centre of a specific culture on a particular occasion in the best society, you do not draw attention to yourself.

Loos's cult of the gentleman can be compared to Le Corbusier's passion for the *objet-type* in revealing a taste for conformism. The stagnation of the male wardrobe was influenced by the determined routines of the bank manager and the civil servant; any impulse for decoration and display was transferred to the dress of women which, in the early years of this century, began to demonstrate an extraordinary variability in matters of taste.

The Victorian idea of the sombre conventional gentleman had its mirror image in the Victorian idea of femininity which depended on what are nowadays dubious notions, such as helplessness, pliancy, weakness and dependency. A reduction in the volume of erotic signals served only to enhance the value of those actually emitted. The wardrobe enforced this, turning modesty into a subtle erotic language. Chastely attired during the day, a nocturnal *décolletage* demonstrated the rhythmic tension between prudery and prurience. Day or night, tight lacing and corsetry and huge skirts

Adolf Loos admired the English style, as did many Viennese. Goldman & Salatsch, for whom Loos designed a beautiful shop, describe themselves in English in his radical newsletter *Das Andere*.

constrained movement and independence.

In this fashion system there was some room for change, but an innovation like the crinoline which was momentarily liberating was soon turned into another impediment. Designed to replace the layers of padded petticoats used to create an absurd version of the desired female shape, the crinoline was a bell-shaped steel construction (whose fabrication reflected other Victorian achievements in engineering) within which women's legs could move freely for the first time in centuries. But it soon grew to exaggerated and restrictive proportions. Heaving and swaying with every bodily movement, it represented both the theory and the practice of the unapproachable, unavailable woman.

Function is a matter of taste

The popularity of crinolines is powerful evidence of the taste for images. At the same time, the cult of Byron and the French conquest of Algiers had made zouave trousers familiar in countless engravings and popular paintings. In New York in the 1840s Amelia Bloomer added a radical and functional element to this fashion with her emancipated baggy trousers, designed to combine practicality with an alternative image of femininity. Bloomers were only the first and most famous attempt to reform clothing.

Although many gestures in fashion have had a functional origin, a reappraisal of clothing on technical grounds had to wait upon the moral certainties and technical ingenuity (and not a little quackery) of the later nineteenth century. For reasons we have seen, dress is much more than mere function, and disposing of the weight of custom and practice in favour

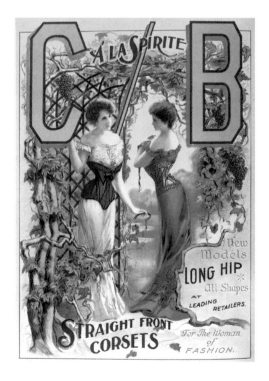

Above The female form is not natural, but a response to fashion. Materials technology complements it, producing depressions, implosions and extensions reflective of the sexual tension of restriction.

Left One invisible, but fundamental, aspect of mass-consumption was that underwear developed style and image in pursuit of sales.

of technical norms required a revolution in values which, despite the zeal of the reformers, was not – and is still not – forthcoming.

As early as 1834 Andrew Combe had published his *Principles of Physiology* in which, for the preservation of health, he argued for the development of physical education to promote clothing that was 'artistic, hygienic and rational'. There was obviously a latent demand because fourteen editions appeared in less than twenty years. Combe was in the scientific vanguard of dress reform, being particularly exercised about the maintenance of body temperature and the condition of the skin. His anxieties focused on tight bodices:

Not only is the insensible perspiration injudiciously and hurtfully confined, but that

Amelia Bloomer, whose underwear liberated millions.

free play between the dress and the skin, which is so beneficial in gently stimulating the latter by friction at every movement of the body, is altogether prevented, so that the action of the cutaneous nerves and vessels, and consequently the heat generated are rendered less than what would result from the same dress worn more loosely.

From the Goncourts to Flaubert, George Sand to Gaston Leroux, remembrance of smell has been used as a literary device. This is perhaps not unrelated to the popularity of perspiration as a technical subject during the same period. Reformers and sanitarians, dedicated to the proposition that wool was better close to the skin, were faced with the battle of convincing the public to abandon 'fashion' for the sake of their health. South Kensington's International Health Exhibition of 1884 was the epiphany of the movement. E. W. Godwin, the arts and crafts furniture designer, gave a lecture on 'Dress and Its Relation to Health and Climate', claiming that

> As Architecture is the art and science of building, so Dress is the art and science of clothing. To construct and decorate a covering for the human body that shall be beautiful and healthy is as important as to build a shelter for when so covered that shall be beautiful and healthy . . . Beauty without health is incomplete. Health can never be perfect so long as your eye is troubled with ugliness.

Perhaps the most remarkable exhibitor was Gustav Jaeger, a professor of Zoology and Physiology at Stuttgart University and an expert on confusing morality with taste. George Bernard Shaw, who was one of his followers, had remarked that 'good taste' was another expression for moral cowardice. His own point of view was, of course, in itself an expression of taste: to Shaw, the major challenge of the era was to establish a simple and rational way of life. Shaw was a fringe member of the health and common-sense lobby. Like Mrs Bloomer, it was driven by a taste for simplicity that was entirely original in Western culture and found expression in many different areas of life, clothing being only the most obvious. Into this reformist milieu came the astonishing Dr Jaeger with his book *Health Culture* (1884) arguing that animal fibre is healthier than vegetable material because it facilitated – he did not say how – the exhaust of noxious bodily vapours. Dr Jaeger was discovered by a London accountant, Lewis Tomalin, whose wife had taught him German. His own best advertisement, Jaeger claimed that wearing wool (as opposed to, say, silk, which he stigmatized as the excreta of worms) had cured him of obesity, haemorrhoids and indigestion.

The demands made on his followers were substantial: the 'Woolleners' wore specially designed wool hats and digital socks. None the less, Tomalin was such an effective publicist of Jaeger's theories that in October 1884 *The Times* published a leader on 'Dr Jaeger's Sanitary Woollen System'. What started as a private hobby became a cult and the cult soon became a business when Tomalin bought the machinery to manufacture Jaeger's patent knits as well as the licence to use the name on shops. Significantly, one of Tomalin's closest friends was the furniture-maker Ambrose Heal, whose

Gustav Jaeger: a technocratic approach to the problem of underwear. Jaeger's permeable knitwear was a political statement, as expressive of advanced taste as socialism or bicycling.

own designs were an expression in cabinet work of the same simple, healthful ideas which inspired Jaeger and his followers.

Bicycling might never have had such an impact on the taste in women's clothes had it not been taken up by the same fashionable set who accepted the theories of Dr Jaeger. At first this most functional of devices was not treated functionally, but rather as an entertainment. Servants would cycle to parks where on arrival the carriage trade would dismount from their broughams and phaetons and take up the bone-shakers for exhilarating, futile sport. The pantaloons necessary for safe and efficient operation of a bicycle were denounced as shameless, but the women who wore them demonstrated very neatly that taste and practicality could on occasions be united.

The paradox of restricting fashion by reason lies in the susceptibility of the latter to the former. The Victorian watchwords 'artistic, rational and hygienic' are not so much akin to the Vitruvian virtues of commodity, firmness and delight as to advertising's popular trinity: comfort, freedom and convenience. In the same way, the many religious prescriptions relating to washing, for example, show that ideas about cleanliness are also culturally conditioned, which is to say, they are matters of taste. Appeals to higher authorities in order to validate temporary aesthetic preferences always fail to acknowledge that those very authorities are selected on the basis of local cultural preoccupations.

In one and a half centuries of mass-market consumerism there has been a curiously persistent taste for the affectation of working men's clothes. Once upon a time tough trousers with

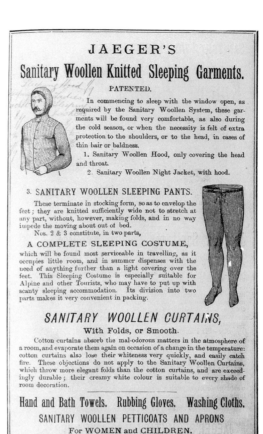

Jaeger's obsession with humours and with fresh air anticipated mid-twentieth century fads for sunbathing and power-walking.

lots of utilitarian pockets made of *serge de Nîmes* were popular among Californian prospectors of the '49 gold rush, presumably for entirely rational reasons. Since then, these 'denims' have undergone a well-rehearsed – and latterly orchestrated – series of transformations from symbol of rebellion to symbol of status. No garment illustrates the fallacious nature of neutrality in dress so much as jeans: dressing down is as conspicuous a gesture as dressing up. Alan Hare, the English proprietor of Château Latour, the first growth claret, affects to wear French workmen's trousers with his very English ties.

From about 1936, when the Levi Strauss

Miners wearing jeans in the 1930s. While fashion has traditionally been inspired by sport or politics, in the twentieth century leisure clothes have been inspired by proletarian workwear.

James Dean's death in a Porsche sports car gave him an ironic claim to immortality. His preference for jeans turned wearing them into an act of sartorial rebellion for the next generation.

company became self-conscious of its own image and inserted the tab on the back pocket, jeans have been more than workaday. In *The Wild One* (1954) and in *Rebel Without a Cause* (1955) first Marlon Brando and then James Dean made jeans into symbols of alienation whose power was not diminished, but rather enhanced, by their familiarity and accessibility. Their adaptability made them perfect material for stylistic innovation both in and out of the commercial mainstream. While skinheads cropped and bleached, hippies attached bells and paisley patches. Jockey launched denim-look Y-fronts for 'executives' who wished to keep their rebellion discreet.

But the biggest pretence was the idea that

wearing jeans was not really dressing at all, merely a value-free decision not to be naked. Of course, the very notion of sartorial egalitarianism is flawed. At this moment the fashion industry intervened and with the 'designer' jeans avenged itself on hypocritical notions of normalcy, allowing the total victory of consumerism and exposing the fragility of functionalism as applied to fashion. Umberto Eco has often pointed out that any garment which grips a man's testicles is bound to have a moderating influence on his behaviour and deportment – to say nothing of his appearance. Thus, the popularization of jeans has forced men to realize something women have always known: that exterior appearance influences, even if it does not reflect, the interior life.

The relationship between exterior and interior is intimate and intense, but not straightforward. The degree of permissible affectation is hard to define, but, like seeing through clothes, impossible to ignore: a man is under suspicion if he cares too much and if he cares too little about his appearance. As Castiglione knew, an impression of effortlessness is attractive, but elusive, and requires a great deal of effort. 'You are what you wear' is, after all, an observation, not a creed. But in the past decade when 'lifestyle' has been more remorselessly marketed and more enthusiastically consumed than ever before, the collective neurosis of a generation that failed to make this distinction has become fascinatingly clear – at least in America's better shopping malls.

Ralph Lauren is conspicuously successful at marketing dressing up for the late-twentieth-century urban man and woman. He owns 90 per cent of the company that sells $600 million

The History of Blue Jeans

1829 Levi Strauss born at Buttenheim, Bavaria.

1847 Emigrates to USA.

1853 First Levi's. Strauss switches from brown canvas to *serge de Nîmes* and chooses indigo dye; the name 'jeans' comes from southern French dockside slang for the tough trousers worn by the sailors of Genoa (Genes in French).

1873 Strauss patents his rivets and the arcuate stitching on rear pockets.

1902 Death of Levi Strauss.

1915 Levis Strauss Company discovers Fordism; jeans mass produced.

1930s 'Dude ranches' created by Depression farmers seeking extra revenue from eastern vacationers. Levi's discovered by middle classes.

1954 Marlon Brando wears Levi's in *The Wild Ones*, James Dean in *Rebel Without a Cause*.

plus annually. His business is designing and marketing clothes which obsessively and cleverly articulate the ambitions of deracinated *nouveaux riches*, but he is in constant danger of reminding his customers of the vacuity of their desires. He packages appearances and sells an image of an image, based on romanticized myths about the Wild West and WASP society, sanitizing new money with a pastiche of old clothes, somewhat like Elsie de Wolfe. But the tension which gives life to the venture depends on the idea that money is a necessary but not sufficient marker of status. The Lauren phenomenon shows that if you cannot buy class, you can buy classy things to wear. The irony is that this expert of style is most sold on those very people – sportsmen, English gentry,

Ralph Lauren, who turned a wardrobe of fantasies into a global business. According to Hazlitt, 'Fashion is gentility running away from vulgarity and afraid of being overtaken.'

cowboys – for whom clothes are expressions of a culture and a response to function.

The Lauren story is astonishing, an odyssey involving a devotion to appearances and pseudo-events that would be merely eccentric were it not so successful. His shops suggest that if you acquire style, you acquire meaning as well. The capacity for simulation goes back through the generations: Lauren (born Lifschitz) is the Bronx son of a mural painter who specialized in *faux bois* and could match up more or less anything. He first wanted to be an athlete and only later, as he described it to *New York* magazine in 1985, did he want to be like Hopalong Cassidy. Later still he decided to be like Jay Gatsby. He got close when he dressed Robert Redford in the screen adaptation. 'I wish I had been to Harvard or Princeton or Yale, but I didn't,' he sighed in the same interview. His declared ambition in the 1957 De Witt Clinton High School Year-book was to be a 'millionaire'. Then he wanted to be a history professor – not so that he could study or teach the Pirenne thesis or look at trade in South China during the sixteenth century, but so that he could dress in gum-soled shoes, tweed jackets and smoke a pipe.

It is no accident that Lauren's company markets its merchandise as 'Polo': he liked the suggestion of European style and horsey society and the 'aristocratic demeanour' he thought he saw in Cary Grant and Fred Astaire. As *Forbes* noted in 1986, polo 'was not a well-known sport in the Bronx of Lauren's youth'. He chooses to advertise in large blocks, sometimes up to eighteen pages, because he is selling an image rather than a particular product. Indeed, it is the ads which

Ralph Lauren's clothes are romantic; his versions of the Wild West, of English country house, of safari have become more powerful than their prototypes. His heroic mish-mash of other people's symbols exerts a strong attraction for middle-brow consumers.

create the Lauren image. The pictures by Bruce Weber are narrative rather than descriptive and show safaris, country houses and black-tie dinner parties.

Lauren was after what Brooks Brothers once had, but packaged it more effectively so as to anticipate, appeal to and satisfy hitherto unrecognized longings among consumers. Interestingly, his critics (easily outnumbered by his happy customers) invoke arguments against him which echo the sumptuary laws of Renaissance Florence and England: 'How does a working-class Jew from Mosholu Parkway dare pass off the tribal costumes of the Ivy League as if he owned them?'

The epiphany of fashion as a billion-dollar language-of-objects industry was when Ralph Lauren moved into his new premises on Madison Avenue, thirty blocks north of Brooks Brothers, who, when they started using Dacron, started losing market. He didn't choose 50,000 square feet in a garish marble-ized atrium. He bought the Rhinelander Mansion, accessorized it and created a Disneyland of status-related fashion which now takes its place with the Frick, the Whitney and the other museums as an inevitable cultural stopping place on the Upper East side. For the opening of this midtown shop, Lauren wore jodhpurs.

Perpetually sun-tanned, like his idol John Kennedy, Ralph Lauren is now his own role model. His achievement in creating a role that is entirely separate from the merely functional needs of clothing is a paradigm of the fashion business; his case proves you can become what you wear – at a price.

FOOD

Acquired Taste

Food is the acid test of taste. Dr Johnson said, 'I take it that he who does not mind his belly will mind little else', and Brillat-Savarin (1755–1826), the great French gastronome, has as the fourth of the ten aphorisms which introduce his *Physiologie du goût* (1826): 'Tell me what you eat: I will tell you what you are.'

People who would not think to discriminate about paintings, buildings or music, exercise exquisite taste in matters of food, but it is notoriously difficult to establish how and why. It is said that there is nothing on this earth which is not as much beloved by one nation as it is detested by another; our very preferences about what we eat are determined by social and cultural conditions as much as by nutrition.

While rotten eggs are prized as delicacies by the natives of Brunei and the English upper classes actually prefer their game putrefied, the Navahos find fresh fish disagreeable and the Old Bretons cannot abide hare.[16] Medieval Arab poets sang the praises of *kamakh*, *murri* and *bunn*, condiments made of rotten barley dough now known to contain aflatoxins, among the most lethal of carcinogens. In his book *Travelling Sketches in Egypt and Syria* (1836) Alexandre Dumas tells a story of being required by social convention to eat a dish made of camel-milk cheese, oil and chopped onions pounded into a 'filthy mixture'. This may seem odd, but Eskimo taste is especially curious by modern Western standards: according to L. R. Wolberg's *Psychology of Eating* (1931), 'there is no sight in the world more revolting than to see a young and gracefully formed native girl stepping out of the carcass of a putrid whale', whence she comes with a

Alexandre Dumas, author of *Travelling Sketches in Egypt and Syria*, 1836.

TASTE + AROMA = FLAVOUR

Alan Davidson, 1987

select rotting morsel of subsequent delectation.

Anthropologists have not yet discovered a group which eats everything available to it, even though the rules of nutrition appear to be universal. The distinguished English gastronome, Alan Davidson, was surprised to react with conventional disgust at a feast in Turkey when fellow guests picked eyeballs and tongues from roast lambs. That he recorded his feelings in an elegant short essay[17] and confessed to his exploratory intellect being at odds with his cultured feelings shows just how vexatious taste can be, even to someone who makes it his business.

Apparently Keats dusted his tongue with pepper the better to savour the taste of iced claret, but his contemporaries in France were already serving Bordeaux with a warm napkin around the neck of the bottle to bring out the flavour of the wine. Clearly, taste is influenced by forces beyond the understanding of science. Of the five senses taste is the most complicated because it involves the intellect as well as physiology. In an epic sentence in his paper 'Science and the Experience of Eating', delivered at the Oxford Symposium in 1987, E. G. Richards defined gustatory taste: 'The experiences encountered whilst eating and drinking are mediated by nerve endings in our mouths and noses and modulated by our knowledge, our beliefs, our predilections and what the morsel looked and felt like before we popped it in our maw.'

For this very reason, perhaps, social and cultural factors influence taste more than they do touch or sound. There are only four basic taste sensations which occur in the mouth: sweet, sour, salt and bitter – a gustatory map of the tongue's receptors. The complex taste sensations take place not in the mouth, but in the brain. The only one understood scientifically is sourness, which can be defined as the taste of a solution with a pH of less than seven.

Smell is perhaps even more fugitive. It is considered in the olfactory bulb, neighbour of the temporal lobe, the home of our memories. This propinquity explains the power of smell to excite memory. Richard Llewellyn, author of *How Green was My Valley* (1939), claimed he could smell hens' feathers every time he ate roast chicken. In fact, the meaning of what we eat and drink is determined more by sensation in the nose than sensation on the tongue. Gastronomists and oenologists use the word taste to cover both flavour and aroma. Rough definitions may be useful: aroma is smell, flavour is gustation, and taste – at least as far as the gastronomists and oenologists are concerned – is the combination of the two. While sweetness, bitterness, acidity and saltiness can be scientifically measured, their meanings and our reactions to them are altogether less determinate. Brillat-Savarin suspected that 'smell and taste are in fact but a single composite sense, whose laboratory is the mouth and its chimney the nose'. But the laboratory is built on shifting sands. One simple example of changing taste is the fluctuating demand for dry and sweet. Vauxhall Pleasure Gardens in London, which flourished from 1661 to 1859, provides an example. It was soon a haunt of Samuel Pepys, whose idea of fun was to go there for a stroll, a lobster and a syllabub. Later it was opened up to people of all ranks as well as diarists. Whereas in 1802 champagne was available for eight shillings a bottle, most visitors preferred

The Taste of Wine

There are four characteristics of the 'taste' of wine.

1 Visual
What *colour* is the wine (garnet, purple, flaxen, amber)?
What *physical properties* does the wine have (bright/dull, clear/cloudy)?

2 Smell (olfaction)
The 'smell' of a wine is experienced in two stages: first, there are the volatile odours arising from the still wine; then there are the secondary odours, frequently different, arising from agitated wine.
The experience of smell has two aspects: aroma and bouquet. **Aroma** covers the entire range, including the quasi-olfactory experience from wine in the mouth, where the olfactory-bulb can be directly stimulated via a channel in the back of the mouth; **bouquet** is experienced only by sniffing.

3 Taste
There are only four taste sensations, experienced by different parts of the tongue:

sweetness	front of the tongue
acidity	upper sides of the tongue
salt	lateral edges of the tongue
bitterness	back of the tongue

4 Tactile
Is the wine effervescent, slightly *petillant*, astringent? Does the wine have body?

Adapted from Maynard Amerine and Edward B. Roessler, *Wines: their sensual evaluation*, 1976

'Vauxhall Nectar', containing rum, syrup and benjamin flowers, as their summer tipple. Hock and 'Rhenish' were offered with or without added sugar and, with claret at five shillings a bottle, 'Frontiniac' – presumably, Muscat de Frontignan, a heavy, sweet, undistinguished wine from the plains of Languedoc – was priced at six.[18]

If the taste for dry and sweet changes, so too does the dimension of the appetite. George Musgrave, author of *A Ramble through Normandy* (1855), watched a honeymooning couple at lunch on a steamer near Rouen. They consumed soup, fried mackerel, beefsteak, French beans, fried potatoes, omelette *fines herbes*, a *fricandeau* of veal with sorrel, a roast

Vauxhall Pleasure Gardens. At this pre-industrial mass entertainment visitors drank gin made out of sulphuric acid and oil of turpentine.

chicken garnished with mushrooms, a hock of pork served on spinach, an apricot tart, three custards, an endive salad, a small roast leg of lamb with chopped onion and nutmeg, coffee, absinthe, *eau dorée*, a Mignon cheese, pears, plums, grapes, cakes and three bottles of Burgundy (two red, one white).

Similarly, ideas about fatness and thinness are not absolute. In peasant societies a thin wife brings disgrace to the husband and for long periods of European history over-eating was a familiar symbol of wealth. Even as late as the early twentieth century, at least as described by Vita Sackville-West in *The Edwardians* (1930), over-eating was a ritual. Yet in civilizations where starvation exists as a possibility anorexia is unknown. In the United States it is still very rare in the underclass of urban blacks.

Because cooking involves the conception and execution of an idea, the assembling of functional components into a pleasing whole, it has both a practical and an aesthetic character. This makes it similar to design, a subject which in the past has lent itself to as much moralizing as food (although the real sense of 'good' design is as fugitive as that of 'good' food). When Marcella Hazan says defiantly to her students, 'I don't measure, I cook', it is not a confession of carelessness, but an affirmation of high artistic purpose and personal conviction.

Patterns in cooking are as cyclical as patterns in art and, viewed historically, betray similar characteristics, a period of excess being followed by a period of austerity, and so forth. Elizabeth David's *faites simple* is as much a moral and aesthetic instruction as a culinary

Sensations

The range of sensations a person can detect is surprisingly small:

solid	soft
elastic	crisp
sharp	blunt
thick	thin
dry	moist
rough	smooth

Emil Ritter von Skramlik, *Handbuch der Physiologie der niederen Sinne*, 1926 one, if the two things may be separated, and, as we shall see, an aesthetic instruction peculiarly located in culture. Her conviction that a bad meal is always expensive is similarly moral and democratic (although not to be confused with G. K. Chesterton's happy remark that there is more simplicity in a man who eats caviar on impulse than one who eats grapenuts on principle). The fear of simplicity which Mrs David says undermines Britain is itself a subtle and fascinating matter of taste whose background this chapter will try to explore.

While any general discussion of taste follows a wandering path between prescription and philosophy, it is perfectly possible to talk about the historical development of taste in French culture. Here, more than anywhere else, very self-conscious and very influential styles of eating first emerged. Luxury is anything in excess of what is merely necessary for survival. In his book *Economy and Society* (1922) Max Weber provided a definition: ' "Luxury" in the sense of a rejection of the purposive-rational orientation of consumption is, to the feudal ruling-class, not something "superfluous" but one of the means of its social self-assertion.'

French cuisine may be a luxury, but it is perhaps in French cooking that the very idea of 'good taste' first appears. Significantly, its first connotations were social and directed against proletarian or peasant values and in support of bourgeois ones. This sort of improved taste was definitively that of the improving grandee: in Molière's *L'Avare* (1682) the despised meanness of the lower orders provides the setting. Three successive titles offer evidence of this trend: La Chapelle's *Le Cuisinier moderne* (1733), Menon's *La*

Elizabeth David: food as workaday Mediterranean romance. To a generation born in post-war Britain there is nothing – in art or literature – as moving as Mrs David's enthralling accounts of garlic, oil and lemon. Her recipes work well in the kitchen, but her real power is in the imagination.

Cuisinière bourgeoise (1746) and Mme Merig-
ot's *La Cuisinière républicaine* (1790s).
Clearly, a process of social orientation is at
work in the titling of cookery books.

The fact that cooking and eating were
becoming another aspect of social competition
is demonstrated by the tendency, which accel-
erated after the Revolution but was present
before it, to name dishes after the chefs or their
patrons. It began when the Marquis d'Uxelles
donated his name to the dish of quails in a
mushroom sauce which is still known as *cailles
à la duxelles*. Louis XV prepared his own ome-
lettes and *les filets de volaille à la bellevue* was
named by its creator, Madame de Pompadour,
after one of her favourite houses. Thus were
social distinctions conferred on certain dishes
and architectural taste and food interestingly
mixed. This process of distinguishing 'designs',
now applied to everything not just food, is
known as the valorization of surplus.

Three great chefs exemplify the development
of French cuisine up to the beginning of our
own age: La Varenne (once employed by the
Marquis d'Uxelles), Carême (once employed
by the Rothschilds in Paris and at Ferrières)
and Escoffier (chef at London's Savoy and elsewhere). French cuisine was initially influenced
by Italian cooking (brought to France by
Catherine de Medici, consort of Henri II). In
La Varenne's *Le Cuisinier françois* (1651) a
distinctive national French cuisine emerges
from a common European medieval inheritance. La Varenne was the first of those cooks
responsible for turning the artisan craft of
cooking into the art of gastronomy, and in the
course of doing this laid patterns of behaviour,
ideas about manners and assumptions about

Antoine Carême, the Prince Regent's chef, who
specialized in amazing confectionery set pieces such as
'The Ruins of Antioch' and 'Chinese Hermitage'.

the cultural role of food which have not yet been seriously challenged.

La Varenne was a *marmiton*, or saucepan boy, in the kitchens of the Duchesse de Bar, Henri IV's sister. It was Henry IV who said that in his reign the poor should be able to have a chicken every Sunday (the famous *poule au pot*). *Le Cuisinier françois* was the first systematic cookbook, an influential refinement of traditional practice. The subtitle reveals something of the burden of the author: '*Enseignant la manière de bien apprêter et assaisonner toutes sortes de viandes grasses et maigres, légumes, pâtisseries et autres mets qui servent tant sur les tables des Grands que des particuliers.*'

But to his followers and critics La Varenne was vulgar and rustic; there is much in his book which carries the medieval sense of awe and wonder, to say nothing of sorcery. He used spices more sparingly than his medieval predecessors, but still savoured contrasts that are to us odd. He insisted, for instance, on adding sugar to meat dishes. His recipe for capon pie:

Take the white meat of a capon and chop it fine. Mix with it two egg yolks, fresh butter, salt, pistachios, and a lot of sugar. If it is too dry, dampen it with a little bouillon. After that, make a very fine, sweet, puff pastry. Line a pie dish with some of it. Put your stuffing into the dish and add some dried currants.

His critics said that what they were looking for in their cuisine was refinement, delicacy and 'good taste', and these attacks were perfect little models of the avant-garde's opposition to the establishment, recreated a thousand

times since, but here applied uniquely and importantly to the kitchen. La Varenne's was essentially a medieval technique subject to modern systematization. In a turkey recipe he suggested slinging on some raspberries 'if you have them'. The transformation that was about to overwhelm cooking and social behaviour around the table was one from 'superposition' (i.e. sugar and capon, raspberries on top of turkeys) to a cuisine of 'impregnation et des essences'[19] – a good metaphor for the manners of the emerging middle classes.

Marie-Antoine Carême, known as Antonin (1784–1833), was abandoned by his parents and taken up by a humble cookshop. His astonishing career demonstrates how social progress could be made both by cooking food as well as by eating it. Beginning as a fifteen-year-old kitchen help he moved to Bailly, the *pâtissier* in rue Vivienne, whose most famous client was Talleyrand. The *pâtissier* taught him culinary sculpture and Carême's most extraordinary creations were set pieces with dishes got up to look like buildings cribbed from designs he had seen in the Bibliothèque Nationale. Anatole France quoted him as saying, 'The fine arts are five in number, to wit: painting, sculpture, poetry, music, architecture – whose main branch is confectionery.'[20] Here we may see the beginning of an impulse, since frequently repeated, to accommodate rogue and trivial subjects into the canon of art.

Carême achieved far greater sophistication than La Varenne. The minor cookery writers of the eighteenth century had, in respectful response to the spirit of the age, included an element of encyclopedism in their books. Carême built on this basis, but added something original: he had clients. As an apprentice he had cooked for Napoleon and was eventually employed by Talleyrand, whose dinners became famous. He then came to England to work for the Prince Regent, he cooked at the Russian and Austrian court, but he met his destiny in the employ of the Rothschilds.

The founder of *la grande cuisine*, he made some claims to universality, but his attitude to his chosen career was specific to his time and to local culture; the sort of sophistication which made him a celebrity was only possible in an advanced economy. Indeed the social transformation which allowed Beethoven to be an independent genius while, fifty years before, Haydn had been a servant, also affected the role of the chef. Carême was an arbiter, an artist, a creator, a taste-maker. Dinner was a painting with chiaroscuro, iridescence and limpidity. He used spun sugar and moulded lard to make his *pièces montées* with palm trees, military trophies, lyres, perfume pans and ornamental plinths straining under the weight of red-legged partridges afloat in his beloved and noisomely complicated *espagnole* sauce.

He explained in *L'Art de la cuisine française au 19ème siècle* (1833–) that it is 'an error for those of lesser station to try to pattern their tables after the rich, crowding them with badly prepared food, badly served because of inexperienced help. Better . . . a simple meal, well-prepared; and not to try to cover the bourgeois table with an imitation of the rich.'

The Italian composer Rossini was a frequent house-guest of the Rothschilds and for him Carême created the vile *tournedos Rossini*: filet steak, *foie gras* and truffles. Another visitor to the Rothschild household, Lady Sydney Morgan, said in her *France in 1829–30* (1831) that a Rothschild dinner was a 'specimen of the intellectual perfection of an art, the standard and gauge of modern civilisation'. In their employ Carême wrote *Le Cuisinier parisien* (1828): 'In this wealthy household, I could spend as much as was necessary in order to prepare things as I wished. This is the only way in which a creative cook can fully profit from his talents, for what good is talent if one doesn't have the money to buy the best provisions?'

This is an apt summary of the vicious constraints of consumerism and strangely reminiscent of Racine's remark that '*sans l'argent l'honneur n'est qu'une maladie*'. But in his cooking Carême achieved a high degree of creative freedom. Completely abandoning medieval contrasts he worked on complementary (which is not to say subtle) flavours. He always wanted to extract in an interesting way the essential character of the food he was preparing. Although Baron Rothschild invited him to retire to Ferrières, Carême refused. It was the rebuff of one *nouveau riche* to another: '*Je lui dis encore que mes livres m'avaient créé un revenu qui allait bien au-delà de mes besoins.*'

Carême was the first truly modern cook and, perhaps more significantly, saw himself as such. His interest in purity was a gastronomic expression of a broader urge in culture as a whole. He refused to garnish meat with fish (a noxious practice which not all of his less skilled descendants have abandoned). His *fonds de cuisine* with the three expensive and intricate sauces provided the basis for 'classic' French cuisine and for a gastronomic culture whose development both Rossini and Dumas (who believed that his *Grand dictionnaire de cuisine* (1873) was a far superior work to *The Three Musketeers* or *The Count of Monte Cristo*) encouraged in their different ways. But perhaps the key figure in this development was not a musician or writer but another cook, Escoffier.

August Escoffier (1847–1935) made French cuisine into an international standard. It was Escoffier who canonized restaurant French by the popularity of his *Livre des menus* (1912). In 1893, following the tradition of Pompadour and Colbert, he created for Nellie Melba the pudding that bears her name.

In 1890, in company with César Ritz (of the Grand Hotel, Monte Carlo) and Echenard (of the Hotel du Louvre, Marseille), Escoffier created the Savoy and thus perpetuated for generations of Englishmen certain assumptions about *haute cuisine*. Part of his achievement was to reject the architectural fantasies of Carême and instil the kitchens of the Savoy with a new spirit so that heavily decorated food did not arrive stone cold and inedible at the guest's table.

But his revolution in the kitchens at the Savoy had more than thermal advantages for hungry, jaded diners. He restructured the operation of the kitchen so that there was a division of labour: thus, with nice symmetry, the new rich of the joint stock enterprises could benefit at table from the process which helped them acquire their wealth. The clientele, newly aware of the concept of efficiency, relished the innovation. In Escoffier's kitchen different divisions carried out different operations, rather than distinct dishes. The structure he established is still in use today:

Right People learn about interior design from restaurants, which reinforce and project our expectations. Restaurant design is in sensitive sympathy with the style of food served. Each articulates a certain set of values.

Garde-manger: supplies the kitchen and prepares cold dishes.

Entremettier: prepares soups and desserts.

Rôtisseur: prepares meats.

Pâtissier: prepares bread and pastry.

Saucier: does the sauces.

The Escoffier period at the Savoy and later at the Ritz was the time when all the grand hotels – Claridges, the Piccadilly, the Hyde Park and the Berkeley – were becoming established, and the first cookery competitions took place. That Escoffier put peasant dishes (such as Provençal potato and artichoke) on the menu at the Savoy and turned them into expensive *haute cuisine* reveals the curious relationship between English class and French cooking.

Carême and Escoffier were not the first French cooks to work in England. Against a background of notorious philistinism (one Elizabethan writer attacked the 'affected gestures' of France and even the knife and fork of Italy), there was always a minority who took an expert interest in cuisine. Queen Anne's physician published a commentary on Apicius' *De Re Coquinaria* and as early as 1665 the curious and erudite *Closet of the Eminently Learned Sir Kenelm Digby Opened* was published. But historians and anthropologists have long laboured to understand why cooking in France and England is so different. While in France it did not take long for the sophisticated *cuisine d'impregnation* to replace coarse medieval contrasts, in England the battle still has to be won. The familiar explanation is that the continued existence of court life in France, at least until the Revolution, encouraged sophistication, while in England with its decentralized

In England, writing cookery books was a field in which women competed successfully with men. Eliza Acton was one of the best, but Isabella Beeton (*above*) was the most influential.

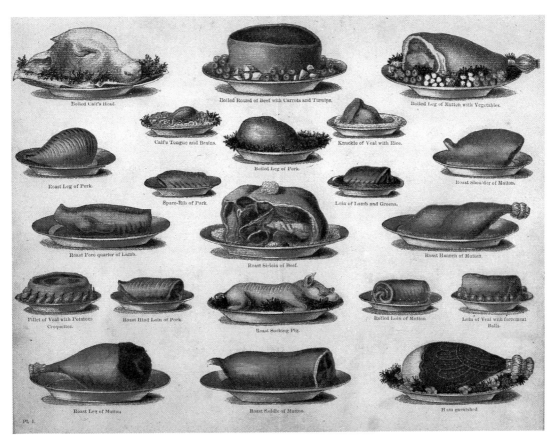

Tastes change: In the 1890s fashionable young French women would visit abattoirs to drink a glass of fresh blood. Mrs Beeton's *Everyday Cookery* presented many choices for carnivores but few for herbivores.

social life, country (which is not to say peasant) values were more acceptable. Simple food was preferred to ostentatious refinement. The English lived on the land and preferred rural models; the aristocracy and gentry in England paid tax, but their French equivalents lived at a rarefied level of isolated privilege.

It is extraordinary that the most famous, although not the first, modern cookery book in England was written by a woman. As author of *Beeton's Book of Household Management* (1861) Isabella Beeton made her husband's name a generic in much the same way as Lux and Hoover. She was twenty-five when it first appeared and twenty-nine when she died, just before the dictionary edition appeared. If cookery writing of the eighteenth century had been encyclopedic, then the most influential cookery books of the nineteenth were concerned with something especially appropriate to the age: scientific management. Beeton's preference was for what Elizabeth David described as sound, solid, sensible, middle-class mid-Victorian food. Much was derived from her predecessor Eliza Acton, whose *Modern Cookery* (1845) was the first English cookery book to systematize ingredients, quantities and timings. Her contemporary, Alexis Soyer, the erratic French chef of the Reform Club, was also a source. Like her other contemporary, the Queen's cook Charles Elme Francatelli, author of *A Plain Cookery Book for the Working Class* (1852), Beeton had an admirable interest in economy. But the synthesis she created out of disparate sources had the originality of genius. *Household Management* is at least as capable of capturing the spirit of its age as a conventional work of art.

Food historians are much exercised by the problem of why certain cultures prefer certain foodstuffs and Mrs Beeton is a determining influence in England – Mrs Beeton the publishing phenomenon, that is, rather than Isabella Beeton, the spirited and independent Victorian original. Successive editions of *Household Management* lost the original clarity and purity of Isabella Beeton's concept and added the editors' own conceits. It is not too fanciful to suggest that the aversion to foreign food endemic in Britain until very recent times – curry, according to Arthur Machen, is 'the most nauseous of all the massacres which go to form English Cookery of our doleful day'

– can be traced to horrible recipes infiltrated into *Household Management* by unscrupulous editors at work for the opportunistic publishers. With copies of *Household Management* in virtually every home in the land, it took two world wars and a social revolution to rid the British of a phobic disregard for exotic food. Fish klosh, roast wallaby and parrot pie from the 1906 edition are perhaps to blame.

National tastes tease scientific analysis because they defy reason. The stories are legion about the curious foreign visitor to England finding that English food is the way it is because of a clearly defined national preference, not because of lack of opportunity. In an article in the *Evening Standard* in 1935 Osbert Sitwell attacked the Wine and Food Society as pretentious. In a 1983 television interview the patrician Harold Macmillan exclaimed that, at least in his household, it was considered bad form even to talk about food.

The splendid Edwardian Colonel Newnham-Davis, gastronomic correspondent of the *Pall Mall Gazette* and author, with Algernon Bastard, of *The Gourmet's Guide to Europe* (1903), was one of the first Englishmen to take gastronomy seriously (although it was characteristically English that he did so as an amateur). He cites Brillat-Savarin as an epigraph: 'The pleasures of the table are common to all ages and ranks, to all countries and times; they not only harmonise with all the other pleasures, but remain to console us for their loss.'

This is the beginning of a European perspective in English cultural life. Enforced by the world wars, it led to the slow awareness that food was a pleasure and that preparing, serving and eating it were pleasing rituals which

carried great meaning. Yet in 1921 it was possible for a gentleman to write: 'An Englishman
will eat anything if it is served hot, there is
plenty of it, and he is sure he knows what it
is. The fear that a designing foreigner may one
day make him eat cat is still present in one
form or another in most British minds.'[22]

The process could be said to culminate with
the quixotic restaurateur Marcel Boulestin
doing cookery demonstrations on television,
the first of their kind. He describes the experience in the second part of his autobiography,
Ease and Endurance (1948). But before
the 1950s there was very little change in
English attitudes to food. The general philistinism about food – confounded with minute

The unbearable depression of a rissole and beige soup
in a grey environment. The awfulness of post-war
British restaurants inspired a revolution in cooking
and interior design.

sophistication in other matters – is frequently
described by Boulestin:

> I remember dinner at an MP friend's house
> – lovely house, superb silver, expensive
> fruit; no male servants, but several parlour
> maids in lace aprons. The white wine was
> so incredibly bad that, pretending to be
> interested in it, I asked its name. My hostess
> did not know it, nor did the parlour maid,
> who went to the pantry to look at the bottle.

Of English waiters he writes,

> Some . . . such as the old provincial waiters
> are not educatable. I saw two superb exam-
> ples. One of them, who served an abomin-
> ably corked Lafitte, confided the secret to
> me: 'What can you expect, sir, when the
> cellarman keeps the bottles lying down so
> that the wine touches the corks?' Another
> time I saw to my great surprise an Yquem
> 1921 on the wine list, and I told the waiter
> to serve it properly cold. 'Oh, you need not
> be afraid here, sir,' he said proudly. 'Our
> white wines are always in a refrigerator.'

That English wine consumption has in-
creased nearly tenfold since the early 1960s,
that the English can now claim to have a better
general knowledge of wine than any other
nation, French and Italians included, is much
to do with the influence of Elizabeth David
and some of her contemporaries. In an article
written for the *Spectator* in 1963 she describes
the conditions in Britain just after the Second
World War:

> It was not feasible, in 1947, to go out and
> buy food as nowadays I would. When you

stayed more than a night or two in a hotel you gave them your ration book, retaining only coupons for things like chocolate and sweets ... Hardly knowing what I was doing ... I sat down and ... started to work out an agonised craving for the sun and a furious revolt against that terrible, cheerless, heartless food by writing down descriptions of Mediterranean and Middle Eastern cooking. Even to write words like apricot, olives and butter, rice and lemons, oil and almonds, produced assuagement. Later I came to realise that in the England of 1947, those were dirty words that I was putting down.

What was required now was not encyclopedic cookery books, nor those about scientific management, but cookery books full of social criticism and cultural modelling. Aspirational,

Left above   The 'full English breakfast' is as rare in Britain and as relevant as Morris dancing.

Left below   A 'British restaurant' in the Bethnal Green Museum, London.

Below   The 'taste' of wine is dictated predominantly by its smell.

Curnonsky (*left*) and Edouard de Pomaine, authors of the scripture of gastronomy. Curnonsky achieved the seductive link between food and travel, later exploited commercially by Michelin.

'I clearly foresee the day when this vainglorious and immoral people will have to be put down.'

Prince Albert on the French, 1860

some might say. The key word in Mrs David's account is, of course, 'description'.

In the age of the motor car, Curnonsky and Rouff, in their influential series *La France gastronomique* (1921 onwards) were genially adding tourism to the list of delights at table, thus creating for Michelin, Bottin, Gault–Millau, Kléber and Claude Lebey a genuinely popular movable feast. Meanwhile Elizabeth David was patiently turning English taste into continental taste. Mrs David, Raymond Postgate, Primrose Boyd and Patience Gray wrought a revolution in English values. The two last named published *Plats du jour* in 1957. Gray had been associated with the

Architectural Review during its heroic period and her treatment of exotic food in this book had at least as much to do with radical social criticism as with what to put in your skillet or *bain-marie*. Just as during the 1950s the Council of Industrial Design urged the salvation of English taste by importing and imitating Scandinavian furniture, glass and hollowware, David, Gray, Boyd and others sought to do the same with Mediterranean food. Their attack on beige food opened a path which led to chromatic experimentation and variety in all areas of English life, not just in the kitchen and the restaurant. Raymond Postgate's *Good Food Guide*, André Simon's Wine and Food Society and Elizabeth David's *Mediterranean Food* (1950) are landmarks in the history of national taste as a whole. Each led to more choice and more discrimination.

Mediterranean Food, the magnificent result of the jottings mentioned above, was published by the avant-garde John Lehmann and 'decorated', in a style owing something to Eric Ravilious, by John Minton, whose familiar and easy pictures seem to anticipate a lot of what was to happen later in interior design. Mrs David had lived in Greece and Egypt; in her attitude to the Mediterranean we can see something of that ineradicable English longing for the south which goes back at least as far as Keats, but is perhaps at its very strongest in D. H. Lawrence and Norman Douglas.

Other influential books soon followed: *French Country Cooking* (1951), *Italian Food* (1954), *Summer Cooking* (1955), *French Provincial Cooking* (1960), *Spices, Salt and Aromatics in the English Kitchen* (1970) and *English Bread and Yeast Cookery* (1977). The

The illustrations for Patience Gray's and Primrose Boyd's *Plats du Jour* of 1957 were David Gentleman's first major commission. Here was a book full of artistic and social suggestions of how life might be. The bistro movement, foreign travel and 1960s parties followed.

ELIZABETH DAVID
A Book of Mediterranean Food

DECORATED BY JOHN MINTON
AND PUBLISHED BY PENGUIN BOOKS

There is a mournful, elegiac quality to John Minton's illustrations for Elizabeth David. To his publisher, John Lehmann, he wrote about 'art needing above all now a relationship to a meaning in our human lives'. He killed himself at thirty-nine.

titles read like the sub-text of the changes in the British psyche during those years. Elizabeth David presided over the late-twentieth-century rebirth of British consumer awareness. She was interested in equipment as well as in the preparation of food; when a shop bearing her name opened in Chelsea it was national news. That you can buy a *demi-lune* in a department store in Lincoln is due to Elizabeth David's influence on English life.

She declared that the kitchen should be 'the most comforting and comfortable room in the house', whereas most architects, still struggling under the continuing and baleful influence of *Existenzminimum*, wanted to do in 1950s kitchens what even the most radical architect had failed to do in the 1930s: make it into a tiny functional annexe. Now the mandoline grater and the marmite moved in to alleviate the formica as surely as ratatouille replaced the gristle rissoles. Of course, it was a small conceptual jump from familiarity with *salade niçoise* to the wholesome acceptance of a Provençal kitchen. And that meant: Habitat.

Terence Conran's Habitat grew out of these influences and was enhanced by personal experience of France.[22] His business now flourishes there, many Frenchmen following the Law of Exotic Validation by apparently regarding it as a French enterprise. The revolution in popular interior design brought about by Terence Conran's inspired eclecticism is mirrored in food fashion.

Michel Guérard published *La Grande cuisine minceur* in 1976. It was the most extreme version of the self-styled *nouvelle cuisine*, although by now it should be clear that 'new cooking' isn't very novel; it is rather a consistent feature in the history of gastronomy and taste. Periods of deliberate complexity and grossness are followed by periods of simplification and lightening – artifice versus authenticity to nature. After all, Rousseau condemned elaborate cooking in his *Confessions* (1782), and Jean-François Revel, in *Un festin en paroles* (1979), wittily and exasperatedly demanded of an eighteenth-century recipe cited by Massialot: '*Faut-il considérer . . . le canard aux huîtres comme une survivance médiévale ou un anticipation moderne . . . on ne sait.*'

Nouvelle cuisine was a supreme artifice. It offered *le monde à l'envers*. The weekly review *Paris Poche* noted in 1978 that the new cooking entailed a curious inversion of standard restaurant French: starters had to be given the names of puddings, *sorbet de fromage de tête*, for instance; the main course deliberately confused traditional appellations of fish and meat, *rumsteak de sole*; similarly vegetables – *gâteau de carottes*; and puddings were given the names of entrées: *soupe de figues*. It is perhaps not surprising that, at least in England and the United States, many restaurants purporting to offer *nouvelle cuisine* also had themselves interior designed to look post-modern.

Most people learn the fundamentals of interior design from their experience of restaurants. Again, the concept of 'anticipatory socialization' introduced by Robert Merton in his book *Social Theory and Social Structure* (1949) is a useful analytical tool. It would be naïve to believe that what one was paying for in every restaurant was the food: the aspiration and the ambience cost money too. Anticipatory socialization is perhaps best explained in terms of drink: most people drink not so much

because of alcohol dependence, but because of the often bitterly misplaced association of intoxicating liquor with good humour and good company.

The modern meal with its carefully structured progress – which has been analysed by Mary Douglas, the anthropologist, in 'Deciphering a Meal', *Daedalus* (1972) – is historically something of a novelty. The debased contemporary formula of starter, 'entrée', cheese, pudding is known in pretentious hotels and bad restaurants everywhere. The result of a progressive contraction of the bourgeois appetite, it is a simplified version of the food symphonies established in the early nineteenth century. A supper described in Zola's *Nana* provides examples of the dishes that were served for each course:

> Soup: the purpose of soup, Carême says, is to 'moisten and stimulate the digestive tube' (*purée of asparagus comtesse, consommé à la Deslignac, crêpinettes of young rabbit with truffles, gnocchi and parmesan*).
>
> The remove: the first solid food (*Rhine carp à la Chambord, saddle of venison à l'anglaise*).
>
> Entrée: meat, offal, poultry, game (*chicken à la Maréchale, fillets of sole with ravigote sauce, escalopes de foie gras*).
>
> Entremet: either a pudding or a fish; a chance to prepare for what is still to follow (*mandarin sorbet*).
>
> The roast: imposing meat dishes (*hot fillet of beef with truffles, cold galantine of guinea fowl*).

Second entremet: vegetables and fruit (*cèpes à l'italienne, croustades of pineapple*).

Dessert: defined by Jean-Paul Aron in *Le Mangeur au XIXème siècle* (1973) as 'the counterpart to the soup. It was the task of the latter to create the right atmosphere; it is for the dessert to soften the blow of departure, that plunge into the void which engulfs the eaters until their next indulgence.'

Until about 1860 this bewildering array was presented not sequentially, as it would be today, but virtually simultaneously, or at least in three broad sequences: soup, removes and entrées; roasts and entremets; dessert. This, a survival of the medieval fashion of serving fish,

From the Middle Ages to the nineteenth century, all the dishes in any meal were placed simultaneously on the table.

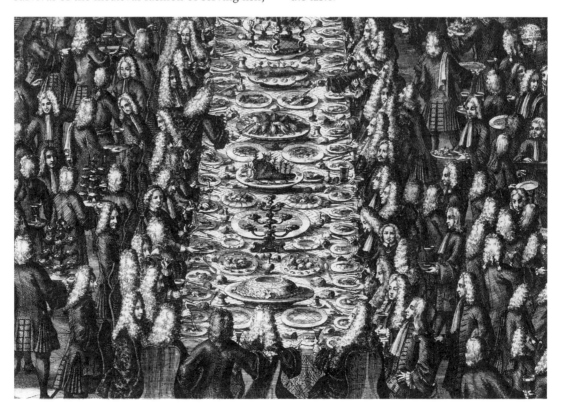

flesh and sweet pell-mell, is known as *service à la française*.

This was superseded by *service à la russe*, which has some very important distinctions peculiar to modern, democratic societies: carving is done in the kitchen, or at a *guéridon*, or, at home, on a sideboard; waiters serve the diners, who are expected to eat something of every dish. The free-for-all of *service à la française* is replaced by the more uniform, but more manageable, linear process of succession which has proved more durable.

The service and presentation of the food communicate the abstract ideas underlying the menu to the consumer. Grimod de la Reynière (1758–1838) established the norms. He declared for the benefit of bourgeoisie that napkins should be genteelly placed on laps, not stuffed manfully into collars; that the fork should be on the left and the knife and spoon on the right; that there should be a variety of glasses for different wines and water. It was expected throughout the nineteenth century that cutlery and crockery should be replaced for each course. This failed to happen in only the humblest homes. In the grandest, a virtue was made of profligacy: the French Rothschilds owned a dinner service and a vermeil dessert service consisting of 112 pieces.

It is usually assumed that the French eat out more than the English, but this is in fact difficult to corroborate.[23] According to Brillat-Savarin, even in Paris in the days before the Revolution 'the stranger within the gates ... found few resources in the way of good cheer'. But the Revolution put a lot of the aristocrats' cooks on the labour market. It also changed meal-times. Because the National Assembly sat

at 10 a.m., breakfast was served as early as 9 a.m. Dinner, which Louis XIV enjoyed alone in his bedchamber, moved from 2.30 p.m. to after 5 p.m. The new restaurants catered for this fashion. So in France as well as in England the restaurant, which soon became a cauldron of aspirations and assumptions about taste, is a relatively recent cultural institution, a product of industrial urban civilizations.

Brillat-Savarin makes it clear that the restaurant was created for the middle classes who, with fewer resources, wanted to eat like Colbert or Pompadour or Louis XIV. It was only from the rise of the middle classes after the Revolution that dining-room furniture came into existence. Since then, of course, the dining-room and what goes in it has been a consistent preoccupation of the bourgeoisie, as the most cursory examination of home-furnishings magazines reveals. A well-equipped dining room confers prestige by suggesting worldliness.

Restaurants were public dining-rooms. In Brillat-Savarin's account of their evolution, gustatory relish vies with economic expediency. It is clear that the restaurant was something special and new – a custom-made arena for the very first consumers:

Having once come to a reckoning with his purse, the consumer may indulge at will in a light or solid, sweet or savoury repast, wash it down with the best French or foreign wines, make it aromatic with coffee, and perfume it with the liqueurs of both worlds, and all with no limit but the vigour or the capacity of his stomach. The restaurant is the gourmand's Eden.

Private dining-rooms are a theatre where individuals project their own taste and where everybody has a role.

It is clear from Colonel Newnham-Davis's account in *Dinner and Diners* (1899) that the new hotel restaurants were providing for an itinerant and free-spending middle class a great deal of the heraldry previously sported and enjoyed by the aristocracy. He writes of Claridge's:

> The windows are draped with deep red curtains and purple *portières*; the carpet carries on the scheme of quiet reds, and the chairs have morocco backs of vermilion, with the arms of the hotel stamped on them in gold. The white plaster ceiling is supported by

great arches, the bases of which and the walls of which are panelled with darkish oak, in which patterns of olive wood are set. The quiet-footed waiters in evening clothes, with the arms of the hotel as a badge on the lapels of their coats, are in keeping with the room.

The new restaurants also introduced competitive culinary inventiveness. So much a stock-in-trade of today's media treatment of food and cooking, it takes an effort of imagination to realize that the demand for new dishes is, like the restaurant itself, a product of modern bourgeois civilization.

Immediately before the Revolution the word 'restaurant' had the same meaning as *fortifiant*. It did not refer to establishments or institutions, but rather to a liquid concoction – a sort of tonic soup – usually given to invalids. In 1765, in defiance of the tradition which gave *traiteurs* (caterers) sole rights to sell prepared food, a man called Boulanger opened a shop in rue Poulies selling '*restaurants*'. A sign was hung outside his establishment saying '*Boulanger débite des restaurants divins*' (which Larousse translates as 'magical restoratives').

As in many other episodes in the history of competitive consumption, the story of Boulanger's *restaurant* involved a certain amount of imaginative entrepreneurialism. Boulanger wanted to expand beyond mere soup and, although barred from selling ragoûts (a privilege jealously guarded by the litigious *traiteurs*), he devised a dish of sheep's feet in white-wine sauce. The *traiteurs* sued and lost, bringing Boulanger enhanced fame. By 1786, in large part due to the *succès fou* of the vinous

pieds de mouton, the word *restaurant* was appearing in legal documents in the sense we understand it today: it was not a soup, but had become an establishment, and restaurateurs were those tradesmen who made a living from welcoming strangers on to their premises and offering them prepared meals.

A commonplace today, it should be emphasized that this practice was a novelty at the time of its introduction. The very concept of the *table d'hôte* speaks volumes about the social, cultural, practical and economic assumptions of early bourgeois civilization: after all, eating with a host whom you do not know is a surprising thing to do. No wonder that the restaurant soon established all manner of comforting and familiar rituals.

The things distinguishing the restaurant from the *auberge* or the tavern were cleanliness, luxury and the quality of the food. Brillat-Savarin describes the clientele, a nice cross-section of an emergent consuming class: there are solitary diners; out-of-towners; a conversationless couple; lovers; regular patrons who know the names of the waiters; 'a type only met with in Paris, which has neither property, income, nor employment, but yet contrives to spend freely'; and lastly, the tourists who 'cram themselves with double portions, insist on all the most expensive dishes, drink the strongest wines, and do not always leave without assistance'.

Boulanger's prototype was followed by an establishment created by Beauvilliers in 1783. According to Brillat-Savarin, Beauvilliers could recognize the faces and recall the names of his clients even after twenty years. The very essence of the perfect host, he gave an

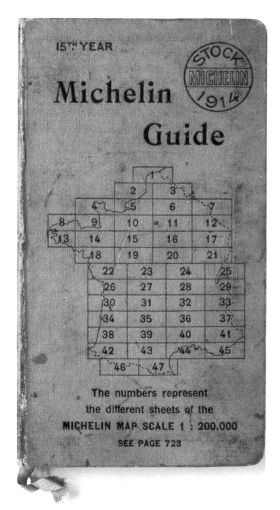

The Michelin Tyre Company achieved the marketing miracle of linking the mutually excitable appetites for fine food and travel.

impression that his restaurant was being opened especially for you. Indeed, the establishment of the 'cover' is evidence of the emerging sense of the individual – eating in restaurants is a romantic experience in more senses than one.

Beauvilliers employed great chefs and was at the service of the new liberal society, at just the same time as he was out to benefit from it. Supply and demand, universal suffrage and freedom of the press were the muses in this progressive game. For instance, in his *L'Art du cuisinier* (1816) he lists thirty-six soups but by 1856, when Urbain Dubois's *Cuisine classique* appears, that number has risen to more than one hundred.

The restaurants that followed Boulanger and Beauvilliers each specialized in one dish – salt cod and garlic at Les Frères Provençaux, entrées with truffles at Very, oysters at Balaine – but the repertoire was growing: before Balaine's Rocher de Cancale closed in 1860, it was offering more than two hundred dishes. The increasing sophistication of the menu suggests that restaurants cannot be understood outside the world of competitive bourgeois consumption.

Parallel with the creation of restaurants is the emergence of the gastronomes, the grammarians of taste, often majestically named: Jean-Anthelme Brillat-Savarin, who was said to carry a dead woodcock and sometimes other small game birds in his pocket to savour the aroma, and his great contemporary Alexandre-Balthasar-Laurent Grimod de la Reynière. The gastronomes were not necessarily cooks themselves, but were certainly consumers. Most of all and most typical of liberal bourgeois

civilization they were commentators and critics. As Curnonsky said, gastronomes rec-
onciled cooking with manners. In his *Considér-
ations sur la cuisine* (1931) de Prescal
explained the role of the gastronome: 'There is
such a thing as bad taste . . . and persons of
refinement know this instinctively. For those
who do not, rules are needed.'

Brillat-Savarin has been quoted to exhaus-
tion, a fine testament to the rich menu of ideas
he proposes. Grimod is less well plagiarized,
but none the less significant. He established the
Jury des Desgustateurs, who met regularly at
the pioneer restaurant Rocher de Cancale.
They produced the prototype of all subsequent
guides: the *Almanach des gourmands*, published irregularly between 1803 and 1812.

The guide, like the restaurant, depends on
consumers.

Curnonsky and Rouff, and later Samuel
Chamberlain, established a relationship
between food and travel. This has helped
broaden expectations of restaurants and their
environments, leading to regional dishes which
Brillat-Savarin might have disdained being
assumed into the culinary canon. But still there
remains the phenomenon of the three-star
Michelin restaurant, or the Gault–Millau
Super Quatre-Toques. Although Gault–Millau
was established as a champion of *nouvelle
cuisine* to challenge the *ancien régime* of cream
and butter championed by Michelin, it is
interesting to note that year in and year out
their judgements about quality tend to
coincide.

The 'best' French restaurants all tend to look
the same and that look is without exception
vulgar. The furniture is imitation Looey

The proletarianization of the aristocratic *bœuf
stroganoff* is an example of reversals which
characterize the history of taste. Nowadays it is more
sophisticated to eat the thymus and the pancreas: offal
is acceptable again.

Above A Paris restaurant *c.* 1900. The assumptions of local French catering dominate the world.
Right A classic French restaurant of today. The language of 'restaurant French', established by Escoffier and others, creates the framework of our expectations; the furniture is its accomplice.

something, with ormolu and gilt. The proprietor's portrait may be acid-etched on the drinking glass. The celebrated restaurants inevitably belong to ideal couples, the woman with a certain hair-do, the man with a fixed smile. Why should sophisticated dishes such as *gigot d'agneau farci en croûte*, which demand extraordinary patience and skill in preparation, be served in restaurant environments of such hideous vulgarity?

The commercial preparation of food by third parties for sale to strangers in establishments called restaurants was, as we have seen, the first experiment in the full-blown consumer service. Since the 1780s the process has been one of continuous proletarianization.

One of the changes which occurred when *service à la française* was replaced by *service à*

la russe was that some discipline was imposed on the consumption of wine: there was no compromise with its quality, but now everyone drank the same vintage. This indulged form of egalitarianism was perfectly suited to a new age where the entire population above the poverty line had the economic resources to choose the services or commodities offered them.

Bœuf stroganoff, named after a Russian prince, is now frozen, freeze-dried and available in restaurants where they print (but do not speak) restaurant French; it has become a proletarian dish. Donald Trump once offered guests *noisettes* of Texas Roebuck Deer with heart of artichoke, chestnut purée and pumpkin polenta, thus completing the circle between peasant and vulgar.

This process applies to personalities as much as to dishes. Imagine a provincial French restaurant, where the young cook struggles to achieve his first star. Yet more heroic endeavours are required to achieve two. By the time the Parnassus of three rosettes is achieved and the first articles appear in American 'gourmet' and travel magazines, the standards which got him there have been abandoned as surely as he has been abandoned to the media. At Le Moulin des Mougins near Nice, as in some other three-star French restaurants, you have to walk through a shop selling the chef-patron's branded tea-towels and oven gloves before you are shown to your expensive seats. The experience is, perhaps, only an obvious extension of the consumerist experience. In *Myself, My Two Countries* (1936) Marcel Boulestin recalled his youth in Périgord and in so doing captured the associational element which is inseparable from the perception of quality in food:

> There were the baskets of fruit, perfect small melons, late plums, under-ripe medlars waiting to soften, peaches, pears hollowed out by a bird or a wasp, figs that had fallen of their own accord, all the fruits of September naturally ripe and sometimes still warm from the sun. Everything in profusion. It is no doubt the remembrance of these early days which makes me despise and dislike all *primeurs*, the fruit artificially grown, gathered too early and expensively sent, wrapped in cotton wool, to 'smart' restaurants.

There is more choice and meaning in the selection, preparation and consumption of food than in any other activity. Brillat-Savarin was correct: tell him what you eat and he will tell you what you are. Tell him *where* you eat and the conclusion will be the same.

None of the innovations of 1980s cooking has joined the repertoire of *coq au vin* or *raie au beurre noir*, but the restaurants designed to accommodate faddish eating habits in New York and London epitomize the consumerist frenzy of a decade committed to consumption.

THE SPORT
OF THINGS

People whose most active form of exercise is jumping to conclusions are too exhausted to come to terms with taste. The idea that we have proclivities formed by our upbringing or our education and that these proclivities distinguish us – for good or for bad – from our fellows is rendered no less harrowing by the fact that it is central to the life of the modern consumer. New communications techniques, mass markets, new technologies have made all things available to all men – at a price. Global advertising by ever bigger networks in the service of ever fewer multinational corporations has turned the world into a shop, but what to choose? When anything goes it is perhaps not surprising that so often very little does. Never before has there been such a democracy of choice; never before has there been such inhibition and confusion.

Does taste have any meaning today? Investigate the newspapers and you see that there is a feeling, to put it no higher, that such a thing as national taste does exist and that the influence of certain events and personalities can either advance or retard it as if it were a current. There is considerable evidence that occasionally individuals – such as Coco Chanel, Elsie de Wolfe, Elizabeth David, Kenneth Clark or Ralph Lauren – with a sense of style or purpose in fashion, interior design, cooking or art appreciation influence their own and subsequent generations. On the basis of their proclivities, public expectations are formed. In this sense there are indeed tastemakers, but the assumption underlying most journalistic comment is that good or bad taste exists independently, and that the art, literature, architecture, design, food or manners of

Hard noses do not make strong principles. Couture, especially Chanel's, was an act of elegant rebellion. Anna Wintour, editor of US *Vogue*, is typical of slavish customers who have turned an irreverent fashion into a dead uniform.

any particular moment can be judged against some ill-defined or unarticulated standard established at some unspecified point in the past. This feeling presupposes the existence of an idealized notion of excellence – even if it sounds absurd to say something so high-falutin in so irredeemably low-falutin an area as popular journalism.

But the influence of impressive individuals in imposing, or at least offering, their own taste to the rest of us has to be judged against the sempiternal observation that there are no fixed standards in art or behaviour. For instance, in his *Manual of Diet in Health and Disease* (1875) Thomas King Chambers had this to say about the dangers of garlic:

> Another article that offends the bowels of unused Britons is garlic. Not uncommonly in southern climes an egg with the shell on is the only procurable animal food without garlic in it. Flatulence and looseness are the frequent results. *Bouilli*, with its accompaniment of mustard sauce and water melon, is the safest resource, and not an unpleasant one, after a little education.

Nowadays we are more inclined to agree with the views of Elizabeth David. Seminal is an abused term, but Mrs David's *Mediterranean Food* (1950) was a genuinely seminal book, containing in its brief 191 pages a *vademecum* for an entire generation. In her Introduction she quotes Marcel Boulestin: 'It is not really an exaggeration to say that peace and happiness begin, geographically, where garlic is used in cooking.'

Again, today the last word in the absurdly sophisticated culinary refinements of Californian cuisine are baby pizzas with gossamer goats' cheese, sushi made of foetal fish, demineralized mineral water, Perrier and soda. Yet when President Benjamin F. Harrison had lunch at Sutro Heights on 12 April 1891, he ate the following: oysters and beef tea with California Riesling, Rüdesheimer and Sauterne; cold turkey, goose, ham, tongue, goose liver, sardines, sardelles, caviar, asparagus and artichokes with Zinfandel; sweetbreads with mushrooms (an intermediate course) with Château La Rose; roast chicken and duck with Château Lafite; followed by sponge cake, wine jelly, ice-cream, macaroons and strawberries with Sauterne, Champagne, Cognac and Chartreuse.

The history of wine also shows that taste in the gustatory sense is not constant. Patterns of wine growing, no less than patterns of wine consumption, have changed dramatically in the past and will, no doubt, continue to change dramatically in the future. What we now regard as 'traditional' wine-growing areas are in fact the result of a radical redrawing of the French agricultural map after the introduction of industrial standards of farming in the nineteenth century. Before then the grape had been well established in such northerly territories as Picardy, Normandy and the Île de France, which, during the Middle Ages, were producing some of the most respected wines, but in the nineteenth century it retreated south to the Loire and east to Chablis. Never mind that Dom Pérignon's historic discovery of sparkling wine at the Abbey of Hautvilliers has a specific date; medieval scholars make no mention of *any* wines of Champagne.

Human behaviour is no less variable. It is presently fashionable, as well as highly desirable by contemporary standards, to revile child pornography, except when it is written by effete intellectuals. Jean Cocteau's *Le Livre blanc* (1928) contains passages such as this:

> This boy, who for me represented good luck, bore on his chest the words PAS DE CHANCE tattooed in blue capital letters . . . Was it possible! With that mouth, those teeth, those eyes, that belly, those shoulders, those iron muscles . . . with that fabulous little underwater plant, lying dead and crumpled on the moss, which unfolded, grew bigger, reared up and threw its seed far away as soon as it found the element of love.

This is hardly distinguishable from the sort of filth you can find on the highest shelves of the bookstore at Copenhagen airport in shrink-wrapped packets. Walter Killy made a similar point in *Deutscher Kitsch* (1962), where he produced a fascinating pastiche by mixing purple pulp fiction with a little bit of Rainer Maria Rilke. In the context, the lines of Rilke were undetectable. Umberto Eco did exactly the same in his *Opera aperta* (1962); sentences taken at random from D. H. Lawrence, appear grotesque.

But it is not only the value of specific works of art that changes, it is also the significance of any given genre. Gore Vidal wrote:

> As a source of interest for the serious, film has replaced the novel as the novel replaced the poem in the last century . . . The half-serious reader of yesteryear is now the film-buff. The 'educated' – that is, functionally

Jean Cocteau, who said, 'I lie to tell the truth'. A mass of contradictions, *un homme sérieux*, but one capable of supreme frivolity, Cocteau hid a taste for pornography beneath the respectable carapace of literature.

literate – public looks at television a great deal and reads many magazines and newspapers. They read few novels . . . If a new novel is highly praised it might be consumed by five thousand readers. Edna Saint Vincent Millay's verse used to be read in greater quantities.[24]

All these examples should teach us to be cautious about assuming that the current status quo has anything more than temporary significance, but the examples concerning literature also teach us something else: that in making judgements today we are constantly having to come to terms with the mass market.

The fact that mass markets tend to homogenize our preferences, while people with style may prefer to break away from them, makes taste both a totem and a taboo. There is a residual feeling that 'good' taste is necessarily exclusive: dimbulbs who still believe in it find the idea of the mass market repulsive. The couturier Balenciaga would reputedly, without regard to function, performance or starving millions, spend thirty-six hours without food, drink or sleep, the better to fashion an armhole. He lived long enough to witness the arrival of *prêt-à-porter*, which should, at least in theory, have made his prodigious technical skills available to a larger audience, thereby enhancing the gross volume of appreciation upon which creative vampires nourish themselves. His reaction to the opportunity of creating fine clothes at moderate prices was not to welcome the democratization of luxury, but to condemn the proletarianization of culture. '*Je ne me prostitue pas*,' he said. Kitsch may be a type of art which lacks any value except popularity, but that is not to say that everything which is popular needs to be kitsch.

In *Ways of Seeing* (1972) John Berger noted that the creation of new reproduction technologies, not just *prêt-à-porter*, suddenly made art of any type 'ephemeral, ubiquitous, insubstantial, valueless, free'. That was the whole point of the modernist adventure, which from the distance of the 1990s we now regard as a tragic failure. The story of twentieth-century taste is marbled with the history of modernism, itself a sort of high-minded form of consumerism. Its purpose was to democratize luxury by the application to technology and social engineering to fundamental human needs, as well as to art. Either in the breach or the observance, the modernist aesthetic has been the one fixed point in a story of art and manners which leaps and swerves confusingly. The abstract painters, severe prophets of a new objectivity, believed

A Balenciaga evening dress, 1967.

they had discovered an absolute. Piet Mondrian, for instance, believed that all human expression could be contained in a rectilinear grid of primary colours. Nowadays, as Lord Leighton's reputation rises, we await a revival of commercial interest in mawkish Victorian history paintings.

The idea that history is a linear process which necessarily ends with modernism is now considered quaint. We may have been brought up to despise suburban villas, but we can see more clearly that they provided a real need. James Richards remarked on it first in *Castles on the Ground* (1946). The modernists overstated a case in order to be heard; now that we are more liberal, not to say promiscuous, the history of art has become a supermarket of effects. Styles which once belonged to a certain

The first modern department stores appeared in Paris. Described by Zola as 'cathedrals of business', they began a century of mixed metaphors and literals in the history of consumption. Their cultural aspirations are reflected in names suggestive of literature: Au Pauvre Jacques (*below*); Au Coin de Rue (*right*).

historical period, dishes which were once the privilege of kings and courtiers, paintings which were the property of popes, are the common currency of an extraordinary age when, with everything accessible, there is unprecedented uncertainty about what things mean.

It is an age of material prosperity and poverty of faith. It is the best of times and it is the worst of times. Everything is for sale. Not for nothing did the Victorians use the word 'spend' to suggest sexual excess as well as profligacy in consumption. Shopping is one of the chief cultural experiences of the late twentieth century. The Duchess of Windsor once said she would prefer to shop than eat, a preference memorialized at her funeral service, where the flowers surrounding her emaciated corpse came predominantly not from mourning individuals but from the boutiques of Dior, Van

Cleef, Alexandre and other jewellers and couturiers. 'So much,' said novelist Dominick Dunne 'for style.'

Freedom of choice has not created conditions of universal ease in matters of consumption, but rather the opposite: inhibition is, apparently, a stronger force than extravagance when consumption betrays the character of the soul. Taste is a new religion whose rites are celebrated in department stores and museums, two institutions whose origins lie in exactly that historical period which witnessed the explosion of popular consumption.

The department store rose with the middle-class consumer and each helped define the other. The range of merchandise and the hierarchies into which it was organized helped create a notion of middle-class normality which even today is difficult to escape. To many people brought up near Harrods, stationery has an ineradicable connection with perfumery in the landscape of their imaginations. Pets are related to hi-fi for the same reasons. Here, for the first time, there was the opportunity to inspect without commitment, one of the great and unique experiences of our century. In *Au bonheur des dames* (1883) Zola describes the luscious window displays of his imaginary store, but does not comment that window-shopping provided the very first opportunity for *speculative consumption*, a phenomenon which today also takes the form of television advertising and magazine journalism.

While Restoration Paris had several large *magasins de nouveautés*, such as Au Masque du Fer, La Fille Mal-gardée, Le Diable Boîteux, Deux Magots and the Coin de Rue, the department store as we know it is a creation of the later nineteenth century. In 1852 Aristide Boucicaut, who worked in a *mercerie* called Bon Marché in the rue du Bac, decided to expand and in 1869 he commissioned a *grand magasin* to be built at the corner of the rue de Sèvres and rue Velpeau from M. A. Laplanche. Extended by Louis-Charles Boileau and Gustav Eiffel, by 1906 it occupied an entire block and had a staff of 7,000.

In the Bon Marché, Grands Magasins du Louvre, Samaritaine and the Bazar de l'Hôtel de Ville lower prices fostered mass consumption and broadened the customer base. Zola was inspired by the Bon Marché; he calls the store in *Au bonheur des dames* a 'cathedral of business'. In the old shops, where haggling was commonplace, the presence of respectable women would have been unthinkable, whereas Zola saw Bon Marché as a 'temple to woman'.

Gordon Selfridge, the American entrepreneur who gave London its first modern store. He helped transform shopping from a subsistence activity into entertainment.

With its libraries, concerts and fashion shows,
Selfridges offered more than mere merchandise.

Although the department stores helped
create the middle classes, it is interesting to
note that the owner-entrepreneurs who created
them, like Boucicaut, were usually themselves
of peasant extraction. Samaritaine's Cognaq
was an orphan and Félix Potin a small-holder.

Aristide Boucicaut deliberately made the Bon
Marché similar to an exhibition, and, appropriately for a cultural institution, it organized
tours, had a reading room and held concerts.
In London, the greatest attractions of the new
department stores were the elegant but inexpensive restaurants. When Gordon Selfridge
opened his huge store in Oxford Street in 1909
he said he wanted it to be 'not so much a shop

as a social centre', where customers could not only have tea, they could watch a fashion show and listen to Strauss, Lehar or Gilbert and Sullivan. He used the impressive free-style classicism of his Oxford Street store as advertising, using architecture to sell knickers.

Just as department stores are cathedrals of commerce, museums have become emporiums of style. The architect Philip Johnson, who, after half a century of influence at New York's Museum of Modern Art, has authority in these matters, exclaimed that museums are taking the place of temples and palaces in cultures which have abandoned God but still require higher values to defer to – especially, one might add, those represented by money. The philosopher Benedetto Croce once explained that everyone knew what art *was*, but no one knew how to define it. Hence, the connoisseur was brought into the drama of human behaviour, a specialist of refined knowledge who could determine art from non-art.

In 1925 Le Corbusier predicted in *L'Art décoratif d'aujourd'hui* that the museum would cease to be a marble hall with a knackered Apollo and a limbless Aphrodite; the quotidian would be raised to the monumental:

A plain jacket, a bowler hat, a well-made shoe. An electric light bulb with bayonet fixing; a radiator, a tablecloth of fine white linen; our everyday drinking glasses, and bottles of various shapes ... A number of bentwood chairs ... we will install in the museum a bathroom with its enamelled bath, its china bidet, its wash basin, and its glittering taps ... clearly, this museum does not yet exist. Such a museum would be truly

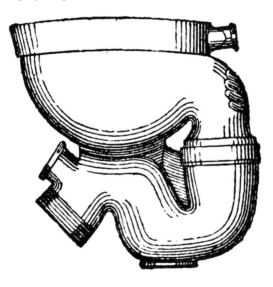

The cool, anonymous perfection of mass-production exerted a magnificent attraction over modernists such as Le Corbusier, who, quite correctly, believed everyday things could be beautiful.

dependable and honest; its value would lie in the choice that it offered, whether to approve or reject; it would allow one to understand the reasons why things were as they were and would be a stimulant to improve on them.

There is a sort of consensus about what constitutes quality in design, what features make a manufactured artefact useful and desirable. You could gather together a collection of department-store buyers, museum curators, Sorbonne intellectuals and consumers, and there might be little serious dissension about what constitutes excellence. At a time when doubt and Utopianism replaced the moral certainties of the nineteenth century, the polemical Adolf Loos, the high-minded Walter Gropius and the maverick Le Corbusier were searching for some sort of order to replace the academic principles which had been thrown out with the *beaux-arts*.

Do the definitions of 'good' design pioneered by the Modernists have a relevance which transcends time?

Respect the nature of materials.
Never force unnatural forms or contrived patterns.
Wherever possible, choose the simplest and most direct alternative.
Ornament is usually reprehensible, but especially so if applied by machine.
Avoid the bogus.
Pay attention to the intended function, which will usually provide a key to the form.
Look to nature and to science for inspiration.

Respect tradition, but do not ape it.
Express your intentions honestly and clearly.
Ensure that the details harmonize with the whole.

There is an underlying substance to the modernist doctrines of 'functionalism' and 'truth' which lend quality to artefacts and buildings as certainly and as surely as classical laws of detail and proportion. John Ruskin believed that inanimate things have a sense of spirit and, in a surprisingly similar way, so did the modernists. The spirit of something pleasingly functional, such as a revolver or a milk bottle, can best be described in metaphorical terms: honesty, integrity, guts and good manners – exactly the same qualities we admire in attractive people.

If quality in design may be defined objectively, 'good' taste cannot. To attempt to do so would be to reduce all the subtleties of human proclivity to a technical formula, rather as if the chemical character and composition of a fine wine, expressed in terms of pH and unions of hydrogen, carbon and oxygen molecules, can in any way account for its flavour and aroma (which, it seems, can be conveyed only by the most poetic allusion). Richebourg '64 is more than the sum of its molecules.

Yet there are times when people recognize 'bad' taste so irrefutably that it is tempting to regard the reaction as instinctive. There are social gaffes, combinations of colours, incongruous juxtapositions, jarring contrasts, impositions of effect, strident appeals to emotion, that most people find discomforting. But, equally, there are examples of exquisite 'good'

taste that are similarly upsetting – Highgate or Atlanta Ionic villas, for instance. Here the proportions may be fine, the colours and materials judiciously chosen, but the effect is unsettling to the aesthetically fastidious.

The answer to the conundrum is where and how an artefact is used. There are few things so discomforting as an exquisite exercise in good taste. You can imagine all sorts of different 'tasteful' interiors in almost any part of the globe. The same pseudo-sophistication will be on show in London, New York, Paris or Milan: holly green walls with eighteenth-century console tables, a turkey carpet; a bathroom with red granite basins; glorious Fortuny stuff hanging from a William IV four-poster; piles of glossy books on fenders and footstools; eighteenth-century prints of Africa glued to Cosmati work panels; Ralph Lauren linen stacked on a bed; more plumped-up cushions than it would ever be possible to use; table pieces; anything with bows, swags or drapes; a Barcelona or Eames chair; tin toys.

These items may or may not pass the modernists' test for excellence, but the judgement of taste in art, architecture, manners, food or fashion depends on the *context* rather than the object itself. It is not necessarily the chair, the swag, the tin toy, the pile of magazines or whatever which is in 'good' or 'bad' taste, but its relations in time and space. It is the intention behind its use. Any attempt to excite respect or any other response by the quickest possible means is questionable taste. Hence our revulsion at the bogus gentility of Ionic columns used on contemporary architecture, or at Savile Row tailors faking country-house atmosphere in their lobbies the better to calm

Left Nostalgia is the eighth deadly sin. It is dishonest, if popular; it shows contempt for the present and betrays the future. Nostalgia demonstrates a crisis in modern taste.

A Savile Row tailors. In the hurly-burly of the market-place there are some fixed values. Paradoxically, the conservative tailoring of the English gentleman's suit represents the same attention to detail and truth to materials that the radical modernists tried to apply to architecture and design.

the excited nerves of rich dentists from Tennessee or zip manufacturers from Nagoya.

Taste is overwhelmingly a matter of personal preference, a person's ability to interpret style or add meaning to gestures, flavours or objects. There are individuals who use their taste to impressively good effect, but when someone else's taste is copied in dress or interior design, the effect is at best derivative and at worst witless. Take Coco Chanel: her artful use of a sailor's handkerchief created a style which Paul Poiret memorably described as '*misérablisme de luxe*'. But the creation of such a style has nothing to do with good or bad taste. As Richard Rogers said,

> Taste is the enemy of aesthetics ... It is abstract, at best elegant and fashionable, it

is always ephemeral, for it is not rooted in philosophy or even in craftsmanship, being purely a product of the senses. As such it can always be challenged and is always being superseded, for how can one judge whose taste is best. . . . Good design on the other hand speaks to us across the ages.[25]

In an age when commerce and culture are coming closer together, it is instructive and amusing to watch the brief, tinselly passage of colourful trash through the spreads of the lifestyle magazines, through the racks and shelves of modish boutiques, while demand for the enduring quality of classics has never been stronger. After decades of uncertainty in matters of taste, simple truths, even simple half-truths, are very alluring.

Taste is not a particular set of values, but the ability to discriminate between things in order to enhance enjoyment of them. Thus, taste depends on knowledge and the exercise of it presupposes an appetite for aesthetic pleasure. In 1273 St Thomas Aquinas wrote:

> Beauty . . . has to do with knowledge, and we call a thing beautiful when it pleases the eye of the beholder. This is why beauty is a matter of right proportion, for the senses delight in rightly proportioned things as similar to themselves, the sense-faculty being a sort of proportion itself like all other knowing faculties. Now since knowing proceeds by imagining, and images have to do with form, beauty properly involves the notion of form.

And, of course, form carries meaning. Edith Wharton said in *French Ways and Their Mean-*

Never has there been so much information about consumption, but never before has the consumer been so confused in matters of taste.

ing (1919): 'The essence of taste is suitability. Divest the word of its prim and priggish implications, and see how it expresses the mysterious demand of the eye and mind for symmetry, harmony and order.'

Properly speaking, design has little to do with taste. Performance, durability, economy and functional efficiency can be measured in a way that approximates to scientific accuracy, but when most people speak of good design what they are really referring to is their own taste. The character of an object is a matter of design, the meaning of an object in use is a matter of taste.

The whole world is a cabinet of curios.

The retail boom of the 1980s betrayed design because it made superficial judgements about a serious subject; instead of being concerned with anthropology, materials technology or ergonomics, design was reduced to momentary matters of taste.

Potentially, everything is for inspection and consumption. In the 1947 movie *Magic Town* James Stewart played an opinion pollster who discovered a town, inhabited by Jane Wyman, which was a perfect microcosm of American taste, full of typical consumers. Now, American market researchers (such as Chicago's Information Resources Incorporated, Time-Life's Selling-Areas Marketing Incorporated and A. C. Neilsen) use computers, cable television and supermarket bar-code readers to monitor consumer reaction to new advertisements. The consumers (who are on a sort of electronic leash) can immediately signal their preferences to manufacturers, while advertisers

The retail boom of the 1980s also produced some remarkable shops, as revealing of late twentieth-century taste as the Bon Marché had been a century before.

The end of design. Engineering and styling have been totally separated and with Japanese manufacturers dominating the technology of consumer products, product design has become merely a matter of taste. Three characteristic European products – a Rover car, an Olivetti computer and a Bang & Olufsen stereo – are all Japanese machinery in Euro clothes. This is the end of a tradition, but an exercise in taste no less revealing of national characteristics than sequins, make-up or a preference for a cup of blood.

can find out exactly what programmes their customers prefer to watch. As an American public-TV producer explained in a 1985 interview with *New York* magazine, 'You used to have an idea, or burn to do a certain series. You'd shop it around for funders. Now you find out what the funders' ideas are and craft their series for them.'

The world is becoming more complicated and never before has simplicity been so elusive. The story of taste is a history of abstraction, from a passive human sense, via capitalization of the initial letter and via industrial capitalism, to a generalized attribute of certain designers or a grail for every active consumer. In an age of popular mass-consumption and global markets, while there are types of behaviour and aesthetic preferences which the fastidious find dismaying, there cannot be the 'rules of taste' which Addison and Reynolds once described.

Taste is not nowadays the same as reason, but as the expression of choice it does have something to do with meaning. Economists are wrong: the law of diminishing marginal utility of goods states that when survival needs are satisfied, the appetite for consumption declines. It is demonstrably a false law. In an age robbed of religious symbols, going to the shops replaces going to church. By our patterns of consumption our tastes are betrayed. It is a beguiling and disturbing drama of ideas. We have a free choice, but at a price. We can win experience, but never achieve innocence. Marx knew that the epic activities of the modern world involve not lance and sword but dry goods.

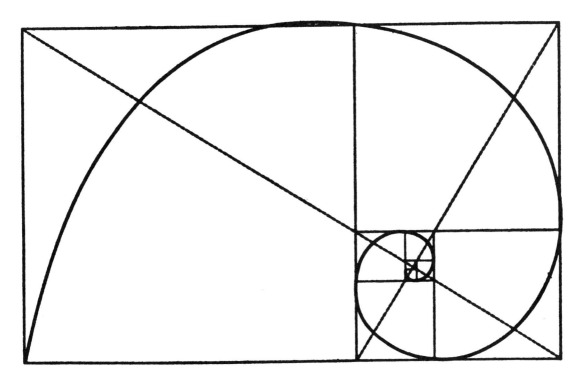

The Golden Section, thought by the ancients to
represent infallibly beautiful proportions.
Approximating to the ratio of 8:13, this is a division of
a line so that the relationship of the longer part to the
shorter is the same as that of the longer part to the
whole. Its basis in the shape of the field of vision
suggests an inevitable biological source for ideas of
beauty.

NOTES

Part One

1 On the relation of taboos to manners and to taste, see Archibald Lyall, *The Future of Taboo in these Islands*, 1936.

2 So too did the German expressionist painter Franz Marc, who compared El Greco to Cézanne in *Der Blaue Reiter Almanach* (1912). Describing them as 'spiritual brothers', Marc wrote, 'Despite the centuries that separate them . . . today the works of both mark the beginning of a new epoch in painting.'

3 Perhaps the most remarkable was Erik Satie, the pianist. A Rosicrucian who had founded the Metropolitan Church of the Art of Jesus the Conductor, he saw in El Greco's *duende* a prototype of the anarchic mysticism he was rather hoping would undermine society.

4 Keats was, in fact, joining a poetic discourse on the relationship of beauty and truth which goes back at least as far as George Herbert; in his poem *Jordan* Herbert wrote, 'Who says that fictions and false hair/Become a verse? Is there no truth in beauty?'

5 Claude Lee Finney, *The Evolution of Keats' Poetry*, 1936.

6 See, for instance, E. R. Curtius, *European Literature and the Latin Middle Ages*, 1953.

7 Some of the sense of taste being related to manners (and of manners being related to restraint), is preserved in the French saying '*Le secret d'ennuyer c'est de dire tout*', a maxim that should be observed by all those reckless enough to

tackle so formidable a subject.

8 There is more of this in J. E. Spingarn, *Critical Essays of the Seventeenth Century*, 1908. Spingarn explains that, to the virtuosi, taste was a 'guide-post to what they sought and a touchstone of their success in finding it'.

9 The document was suppressed by his executors in 1714 and only added to *The Characteristicks of Men, Manners, Opinions and Times* in the 1733 edition.

10 There is an amusing passage in Harold Nicolson's *Small Talk* (1937): 'There are many men who would prefer it to be said that they had acted cruelly, selfishly, perhaps even unfaithfully, than that they were guilty of lack of taste. "Your action", so runs the accusation, "appears to me, and I may say to others with whom I have discussed the matter, to have been in singularly bad taste." One squirms at receiving such a letter.'

11 In a pamphlet by 'Mrs Sidney Webb', *The Discovery of the Consumer*, 1928.

12 See Umberto Eco, *Art and Beauty in the Middle Ages*, 1959; English translation, 1986.

13 P. N. Furbank, *Unholy Pleasures*, 1985.

14 For instance, Hugh of St Victor, *De institutione novitiarum*; Petrus Alphonsi, *Disciplina clericalis*; and Johannes von Garland, *Morale scolarium*.

15 In his *Civilitas* (1560) Erasmus remarks: 'The Germans eat with their mouths open and think it unseemly to do otherwise. The French, on the contrary, half open their mouths and find the German practice rather disgusting. The Italians eat delicately, the French more vigorously so that they find the Italian practice too refined and precious.'

16 The *Independent*, 14 January 1987.

17 Lasinio, *Pitture a fresco del Campo Santo di Pisa*, 1828.

18 See the Preface to *Lyrical Ballads*, 1800.

19 Dr Albert C. Barnes is typical. The fabulously wealthy inventor of Argyrol, an optician's liniment, he was soon on the trail of modern art and ambitiously created a 'philosophy' to support his taste. The Barnes Collection at Merrion, Pennsylvania, became the centre of an education programme based on principles so transparent and scientifically compelling that no one, according to Dr Barnes, could deny them allegiance. These principles included a complete lack of labelling, so as to encourage an innocent response to the art from the visitor.

20 *Ins Leere Gesprochen*, 1897–1900; English translation, *Spoken into the Void*, 1982.

21 For example, Gabriel-Désiré Laverdant, *De la mission de l'art et du rôle des artistes*, 1845.

22 Clement Greenberg, 'Kitsch and the Avant-Garde', *Partisan Review*, 1939.

Part Two

1 In a speech at the Mansion House in the City of London, 1987.

2 *The Architects' Journal*, 16 and 23 December, 1987.

3   Guy de Rothschild, *The Whims of Fortune*, 1985.

4   Ibid.

5   Adolf Loos, *Ornament und Verbrechen*, 1908.

6   Later, Rodker turned towards sexology and psychoanalysis, eventually bringing the Imago Press from Vienna to London and completing the publication of all Freud's works.

7   Ada Louise Huxtable, 'The Troubled State of Modern Architecture', *New York Review of Books*, 1 May 1980.

8   Russell Lynes, *The Tastemakers*, 1954.

9   Ibid.

10 John Betjeman, *Summoned by Bells*, 1960.

11 Elizabeth Hurlock, *The Psychology of Dress*, 1929

12 Recorded in *Selected Letters*, ed. F. Steegmuller, 1980–2.

13 According to the Comtesse de Bradi, 'There is an indefinable element of idleness and flaccidity that ill becomes a girl in the taste for settling down on the bottom of a bathtub.'

14 Rupert Hart-Davis, *More Letters of Oscar Wilde*, 1985.

15 See Robin Gilmour, *The Idea of the Gentlemen in the Victorian Novel*, 1981.

16 According to F. Henning, *Der Geruch*, 1924.

17 In *The Three Course Newsletter*, No. 3, 1987.

18 Warwick Wroth, *The Pleasure Gardens of London*, 1896.

19 Jean-François Revel, *Un festin en paroles*, 1979.

20 Stephen Mennell, *All Manners of Food*, 1985.

21 Lord Edward Cecil, *The Leisure of an Egyptian Official*, 1921.

22 Ironically, another famous Englishman with an interest in France and French food, Sir Jack Drummond, author with Anne Wilbraham of *The Englishman's Food* (1929), was murdered there, as Roland Barthes noted in *Mythologies*, 1957.

23 See Stephen Mennell, *All Manners of Food*, 1985.

24 *Times Literary Supplement*, 22–8 June 1990.

25 Bryan Appleyard, *Richard Rogers*, 1986.

SELECT BIBLIOGRAPHY

Since the idea of taste includes all human endeavour where choices are made, its bibliography is potentially vast, uselessly so. The following includes items which amplify points only hinted at, or perhaps even ignored, in this book. No attempt has been made to include periodical articles or the hundreds of eighteenth- and nineteenth-century works, of no particular originality, which use the word 'taste' in their titles. The editions cited are not necessarily the first, but the most convenient. The place of publication is London, unless stated otherwise.

Addison, Joseph, *Essays of Taste, and the Pleasures of the Imagination*, 1834

Alison, Archibald, *Essays on the Nature and Principles of Taste*, Edinburgh, 1817

Allen, B. Sprague, *Tides in English Taste*, Cambridge, Mass., 1937

Ames, Winslow, *Prince Albert and Victorian Taste*, 1967

Aron, Jean-Paul, *Le Mangeur du XIXe siècle*, Paris, 1973

Barrère, Jean Bertrand, *L'Idée de goût de Pascal à Valéry* Paris, 1972

Bate, Walter Jackson, *From Classic to Romantic: Premises of Taste in Eighteenth Century England*, Boston, 1945

Baudrillard, Jean, *Le système des objets*, Paris, 1968

Betjeman, John, *Ghastly Good Taste; or, a Depressing Story of the Rise and Fall of English Architecture*, 1933

Bourdieu, Pierre, *La Distinction: Critique Sociale du Jugement*, Paris, 1979

Burke, Edmund, *A Philosophical Enquiry into the Origin of Our Ideas of the Sublime and the Beautiful*, 1756

Clark, Sir Kenneth, *What Is Good Taste?*, 1959

Curnonsky (Maurice-Edouard Sailland), *Souvenirs littéraires et gastronomiques*, Paris, 1958

Cooper, Nicholas, *The Opulent Eye: Late Victorian and Edwardian Taste in Interior Design*, 1976

Dorfles, Gillo, *Kitsch: An Anthology of Bad Taste*, 1969

Driver, Christopher, *The British at Table, 1940–1980*, 1983

Eco, Umberto, 'Reading Things', 1976, reprinted in *Faith in Fakes*, 1986

Elias, Norbert, *The Civilising Process*: vol. I, *The History of Manners*, Oxford, 1939

Gloag, John, *Victorian Taste: Some Social Aspects of Architecture and Industrial Design, from 1820–1900*, 1962

Haskell, Francis, *Rediscoveries in Art: Some Aspects of Taste, Fashion and Collecting in England and France*, 1978

—*Taste and the Antique: The Lure of Classical Sculpture, 1500–1900*, 1981

Hogarth, William, *The Analysis of Beauty. Written with a View to Fixing the Fluctuating Ideas of Taste*, 1753

Irwin, David, *The Visual Arts: Taste and Criticism*, 1969

Krestovsky, L., *La Laideur dans l'art*, Paris, 1947

Laver, James, *Taste and Fashion*, 1945

Lynes, Russell, *The Tastemakers*, 1954

Mennell, Stephen, *All Manners of Food: Eating and Taste in England and France from the Middle Ages to the Present*, Oxford, 1985

Moles, Abram, *Théorie de l'information et perception esthétique*, Paris, 1958

Pazaurek, Gustav, *Geschmacks-Verirrungen im Kunstgewerbe*, Stuttgart, 1909

Zeldin, Theodore, *France 1848–1945*: vol. 2, *Taste and Corruption*, Oxford, 1977

INDEX

ILLUSTRATIONS